Praise for Dream Big

I love this book! Craig's easy to follow format and ready-to-go strategies offer an amazing classroom experience for all students every single day. Experience surefire ways to meet learning needs of all students, ensure a quality curriculum and discover how to solve any challenges that crop up along the way. Craig Shapiro is by far one of the most motivational, inspiring educators I've ever met. Craig always adds to every discussion with his ideas that simply make good sense, and are "list worthy". Each one of Craig's lists is valuable and a piece of the proverbial pie. I encourage you to put this new book at the top of your own list. I know you'll be so glad you did! Craig is a master motivator, sure to inspire you and most of all, no matter what, Craig's shining optimism is matched with real-time ideas that work!

— Mrs. Rita M. Wirtz, MA - Author and Former Principal

This book is ideal for new teachers or for any reflective teaching professional who is looking for a reboot. Lots of practical tips and strategies that come straight from the trenches and not from a theoretical framework. Craig addresses so many issues that can be planned for and prevented or ameliorated. He is the mentor that any teacher would want and this book makes his support accessible to all.

— Kecia McDonald - Complex Areas Resource Teacher, West Hawaii

Dream Big

Stories and Strategies for a Successful Classroom

Craig Shapiro

EduMatch
PUBLISHING

These books are available at special discounts when purchased in quantities of 10 or more for use as premiums, promotions fundraising, and educational use. For inquiries and details, contact the publisher: sarah@edumatch.org.

Book title of Craig's Classroom painted by William Tennent High School 2017
Graduates:
Gianna Zaro
Sara Wong
Brooke Simpson

ISBN: 978-1-959347-23-1

I dedicate this book to my parents, Herman and Arlene Shapiro. Unfortunately, both of them passed away before I even considered writing a book about teaching. My mother would have been so proud that I found a passion for education. While she saw the beginning of my career, many great moments were missed. My father, Herman, always encouraged me to take risks, and while he wasn't thrilled that I entered the teaching field, he provided me with guidance and was a genuine positive light.

Contents

Dream Big: How I Got Here

When I graduated from Abington High School in 1983, I had little idea that 40 years later, I'd be finishing a book about teaching. My initial thought when I graduated was to go into the business field. Even though it wasn't something I was passionate about, my father swayed me in that direction instead of education. Towards the end of my first year in college, I vividly recall sitting in a large lecture hall of an economics class. The professor was a teacher assistant with a foreign accent, which was barely recognizable. Among my friends whining about whom they were dating and extreme boredom, the professor mentioned, "We'll be learning about supply and demand curves." That was it; I turned to one of my friends and said, "There is no way I'm going to do this for the rest of my life. I'm going to tell my dad I want to be a gym teacher." He said, "Can I be there when you tell him? I'm sure he'll be excited about your career change."

Dream Big: Stories and Strategies for a Successful Classroom Was Born!

While there are many outstanding books on teaching, I'm hopeful this will be different. As a teacher, coach, and trainer, my background in exercise has helped shape how I view education and the writing of each chapter of this book. Keeping things simple and easy to understand is a core principle that I've used both in teaching and coaching. *Dream Big* is grounded in practical, right-now ways to help you and your students enjoy the school experience.

My goal is that anyone in education can use much of what's written. Excellent teaching looks similar regardless of grade level or subject area. As you're reading, many presented ideas seem like common sense. The practical approach to each chapter will get you at least thinking and trying those ideas.

I've broken the book into three sections: Mission Impossible, When the Rubber Meets the Road, and Look in the Mirror. The core concepts are getting off to a great start with relationships, building our teaching repertoire, and reflecting on their practice. Each chapter has questions at the end to put the words into action. I'd love for you to check out "you can do it" and "get going" at the end of each chapter. They will get you started on Dreaming Big for your students.

Please remember that no book will sidestep every challenge. That's one of the unique elements of teaching; what works perfectly for one person might not for another. With that said, each chapter is meant as a guide, not the end all, be all. I encourage you to take notes on areas you agree with and, even more importantly, those you don't.

For those in leadership positions, consider if your staff is attempting some of what I cover. If they are, that's awesome. Keep pushing that narrative. If not, provide them with positive, straightforward guidelines to get them started. We must believe that better is possible each day. Now more than ever, education offers the opportunity to help our young people Dream Big.

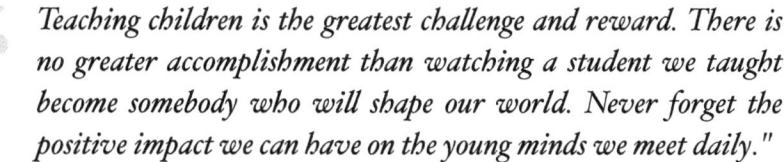

Teaching children is the greatest challenge and reward. There is no greater accomplishment than watching a student we taught become somebody who will shape our world. Never forget the positive impact we can have on the young minds we meet daily."

Foreword

Let's start *Dream Big* with a letter from a former student/athlete, Judy Mabone.

Our relationship in middle school, high school, and even after graduation speaks to the power of relationships and working with young people.

———

I started running in seventh grade for no reason except that no other sport would give me a spot on their roster. Until that first day of track practice, I had never had any athletic inclinations, and for good reason, considering I was slightly below average, I came in the back of the pack during every practice. After the first two weeks of practice, all of that changed when the coach approached me and told me that with some work, I could really be great. I went home and relayed the message to my mother, who laughed and told me to stop lying.

Ten years later, I am a division I student-athlete on scholarship at American University, applying to law schools and navigating the waters of what it means to be a young adult. As I reflect on the past ten years of my life and the many places running has taken me, I cannot help but remember those words of my seventh-grade track coach: "With a little work, you can really be great." The guidance Craig Shapiro has given me over the years, both on and off the track, has been an essential part of my development. The advice he has to offer and the connections he can form with those he aims to reach make him an effective teacher, coach, mentor, and friend.

Craig Shapiro, "Shap," and I have been through a lot together, and I would be remiss if I didn't mention that he knows me as well as I know myself. From coaching me to school record-breaking performances and state championship meets, to training me for a 1:32 half-marathon at fourteen years old, to racing pros at fifteen in road races, and ultimately earning a spot on a Division I team, Shap has always encouraged me to put myself in the race both literally and metaphorically. He clarified that confidence plays a huge role in success in sports and life.

This proved to be especially true when I tore my right hamstring during my sophomore year of high school and strained the left one simultaneously. I spent roughly eight weeks riding a bike while my teammates raced, and the season progressed. My goal of making the state championship for the second time seemed to be slipping away, but Shap assured me that if I believed I could make it, I would. I had to do some incredibly grueling workouts to maintain my fitness. When race day came, I was nervous. How could I, an injured athlete who had just spent eight weeks doing "hill sprints" on a stationary bike, qualify for a state championship meet in a district where, realistically, I would have to run around 19:00 in a 5K to make it? The answer is, as Shap always stressed, confidence. I bought into the idea that I could be great with a little more work, and he was right.

That sophomore season challenged both Shap and me. I still don't know if he genuinely believed I could qualify that year, but if he didn't, he made me think he did. In coaching, teaching, and mentoring, both parties must have full faith and confidence in whatever goal they are attempting to reach, and with Shap, I've never doubted his belief in what the two of us could accomplish. When my faith has been challenged, and I've had every reason to quit, he has believed in me and inspired me to continue to work even if the ambitions I had set were logically beyond what I was seemingly capable of achieving.

The greatest test of this came when at sixteen years old. I was diagnosed with a coronary artery disease that could have ended much more than just my season. When quitting seemed easier than adjusting to my new lifestyle, the words of my seventh-grade track coach rang clear again: "With a little work, you can be really great." Shap never let me make excuses for myself. He never let me take myself out of the race. I remember lying in my hospital bed immediately deciding that my running career was over, and then in walked Shap with an armful of running magazines and a reminder not to eat too much junk food.

Throughout the years, Shap and I have maintained a very close relationship even though I moved four hours from home. When tough times have hit, whether in the form of a stressful workload or, worse, the death of a friend, he has been my first call home. The guidance he has given me over these last ten years has helped shape how I handle life and kept me in the race because it is true that in sports and life, "with a little work, you can be really great."

Shap, I am beyond proud of you for your work on this book. All readers, whether educators, coaches, mentors, or those looking to improve their leadership skills, will gain helpful insight on how to better connect with those they are trying to reach. Your guidance and advice transcend beyond the classroom, and I owe a lot of who I am and how I handle adversity to what I've learned from you. Thank you for your mentorship, leadership, and friendship over these last ten years and for the time and effort you invest in every person you teach.

When I stepped onto that track ten years ago, I never could have imagined your impact on my life. I am grateful to have learned from you, and with this book, I hope that others gain something from your vast knowledge and love for education. I've never met someone who loves his job as much as you do. Thank you for your commitment to bettering your students every day. I hope every reader will gain something from your experiences, just as I have.

With love,
Judith "Dr." Maboné

Section One

MISSION: IMPOSSIBLE

Regarding books, I fall into a "one-chapter" reader category. If I don't get hooked initially, the chances of ever reading to the end are slim. It might seem strange that Stephen King has always been one of my favorite authors. It's not because I love horror but because he is a fantastic storyteller. He easily captivates his readers from the opening page and keeps them enthralled till the end. Even though most of his books are lengthy, I never get bored. His writings are like being in a great classroom; students are excited from the start and look forward to what's coming next. From the door opening when we greet them to the end of the school year when students say "goodbye," there is always something to remember. Like the characters in King's book, each student is different and brings something unique to the class. You want all to succeed and overcome the many hurdles in their path. Students all get to know each other; no matter their personality, they seek a greater purpose. Even though *The Stand* took many hours to read, its initial hook made it special. This is no different from being in a dynamic class. Most students want to be engaged, happy, and connected to you and the other students. Just as I mentioned about being hooked on the initial pages, the beginning of the school year sets the tone for an exciting journey that follows.

As for getting off to a great start when the year begins, I feel it's similar to training a puppy, as odd as that might sound. Think about it: it's unrealistic and hair-pulling to expect your five-year-old dog to stay off of the sofa or not rip up toys if they've never been taught not to from the beginning. Trust me; I've lived this firsthand. Our classrooms are no different. When you're six months into the year and deciding to set class boundaries and a clear message, it still might be possible, but you'll have avoided all of that stress if it had been done on day one. One quick caveat: getting off to a great start does not imply that we should rest on our laurels after the first month. We are constantly pushing the boundaries of risk-taking, being creative, and opening up opportunities for our students. Being persistent and patient will pay off no matter when you try to make changes. While every teacher has a specific persona, if you want to get your students off to a great start, try smiling a lot, laughing a lot, and being happy. You'll be stunned at the positive influence it will have.

This first section has chapters focusing on relationship building, ideas for promoting a classroom of engaged students, and general thoughts on starting the year off positively and meaningfully. Even if you only try one suggestion, the risk is minimal, and the reward will be significant. Of course, many teachers already have and do outstanding lessons to start the year. While I feel what I've shared is practical, positive, and meaningful, I also believe education is only as good as what we accomplish together. Please consider sharing what you use to get the year off to a great start.

· CHAPTER 1 ·

> *Teachers teach because they care.*
>
> *Teaching young people is what they do best.*
>
> *It requires long hours, patience, and care.*"
>
> — Horace Mann

I vividly recall when I began teaching health and physical education in Camden, New Jersey. Despite Washington Elementary having no gym and minimal resources, I was excited to explore the opportunity. I'd met the principal, Mr. Kozieja, a white-haired former armed forces leader who assured me that great things would come my way if I worked hard. He would also end up a good friend and fantastic mentor.

On the second day of school, I took my second-grade class out for physical education. Because we had no gym, all classes met on the blacktop behind the school. The kids were excited to start, and we began jumping rope and doing various relay races. As the class was going strong, a second-grader, Mark (not his real name), yelled out, "Mr. S., the trash truck! Look, the trash truck!" I turned around to see a giant trash truck coming into our area. As the students yelled, juices from the back of the truck spilled onto the blacktop creating a smell that I still recall with vivid nausea. With the kids yelling, "Ewww, it smells," I screamed, "Everybody to the side--NOW!" We moved all the equipment near the wall and waited for the trash truck to pass. Once it cleared, I got them started again. As luck would have it, two minutes later, Mark again yelled, "Mr. S., it's starting to rain!" We hurried into the five-foot-wide hallway, which led to lots of commotion. Because this was a small school, teachers rushed out to see what was happening, followed by Mr. Kozieja storming down the hall!

Fast forward to four hours later. I waited outside Mr. Kozieja's office to discuss the earlier incident. As I worried about what might transpire, Mark entered the office and saw me pacing. He asked, "Mr. S., are you okay?" I replied, "Well, Mark, it wasn't exactly what I had planned for our first day. A trash truck and rain don't make for a great class." Mark assured me with these words: *"Don't worry, Mr. S. I think you did great. Tomorrow will be a better day."*

Why we teach must be grounded in accepting new, challenging, and even harrowing events, like a "trash truck and rain." You could be sailing along, day after day, then boom! Something upsets a lesson, quiz, project, or anything else that might be going well. Please don't let this discourage your "why I love to teach." One final thought on that particular day. In our meeting, Mr. Kozieja said, "Craig, I can see you love exercise and kids. That will carry you through many problems. Please remember, a trash truck and rain won't be the last challenge that occurs. Trust me on that."

Why we become part of children's and teens' lives is one of the most critical questions anyone in education should consider. Even though we may have differences in our "why," I'd like to point out five great potential answers.

FIVE GREAT WHYS:

- We make a difference even when we don't realize it.
- We love what we teach and have a strong desire to share that with students.
- What we do transcends far beyond the classroom.
- We build social and emotional connections that provide hope and guidance.
- We teach skills that aren't just used in school but for many years after a student graduates.

For those who may be curious, my "why" stems from my love of exercise, wellness and the chance to build incredible connections with students. Being able to impact lives in the most positive ways always stays in my mind. Your "why" is probably different but equally crucial for you and the students you teach.

You can do it:

1. What is your "why"? Do students know your "why"?
2. How is your "why" making a difference in the lives of your students?

Get going:

1. If students don't know your "why," please tell them and see how they react.
2. If students know your "why," ask them how it's helped them to succeed in and out of class.

CHAPTER 2
HAPPY

It's the little conversations that build the relationships

and make an impact on each student."

— Robert John Meehan

One of my earliest memories of teaching was at the elementary level. The kids went bonkers—running around and playing a game of partner tag. My initial reaction was, "Wow! This is pretty darn amazing. These kids just love it." Fast forward to my transition to high school P.E., where getting teens excited about sweating at 7:30 a.m. is like climbing Mount Everest. Gone were simple games that kids loved without even thinking about them.

As challenging as that transition from elementary to secondary education was, my preparedness from the gym into the classroom was even worse. I'm fortunate that my supervisor was patient, kind, and supportive. Initially, I thought just showing PowerPoints, providing notes, and presenting rather dull—as I look back—videos would be a great way to teach. Many students were simply compliant in class. Thinking back to thirty years ago, my lack of diverse teaching strategies didn't allow all students to flourish in those early years. Hopefully, reading this will help you to avoid my errors.

While no exact "best method" exists for every teacher, subject, and student, there is a vital distinction between a teacher-centered classroom with direct instruction and a student-centered classroom with a strong focus on cooperation, inquiry-based learning, and, most importantly, empowerment. Teachers who know why, how, and when to use various approaches will meet the needs and interests of their students. Our strategies should mirror a continually evolving experience.

My friend and colleague Dave Fries sums it up here:

"The issue with teaching is that you deal with 1,000 different variables daily. There are only so many solutions to every problem. There isn't a perfect lesson, but there are time-tested ways to teach."

As a lover of acronyms, I use **"HAPPY"** as a guide. It has reminded me of the importance that relationships play in every part of the school environment.

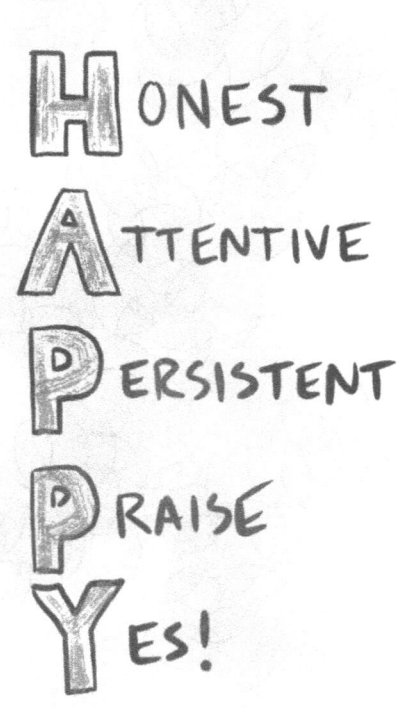

H-Honest: How is honesty related to excellent teaching? Students need you to be honest about how they will be assessed, how the information will be helpful for them, and how you'll provide feedback and praise. Honesty relates well to our "why." Most, if not all, honest answers and discussions should be framed positively. Our initial connections will help you show honesty in a motivating, not demoralizing way. This doesn't mean congratulating a student for missing homework or sleeping in class. Instead, it's developing an open, trustworthy relationship that shows students you're there to help enhance their school experience.

A-Attentive: This is for more than just students. Teachers, staff, and administration, please move around your room, get out in the halls, say "hello" often, and connect frequently. In your class, or even the lunchroom and hallways, please have proximity to students. Being attentive to the needs of each other isn't just about excellence in the classroom; it's also about fostering a focused culture in school.

Simple is often better; start by moving around your room and answering/asking questions frequently. Demonstrate to students that you're interested in hearing their voices. Habitually sitting at a desk, away from students, rarely establishes a positive classroom space. The distance, whether physical or emotional, impacts learning. Even when your attention seems unimportant (silent reading, student research, during a quiz, etc.), all of our time together carries value. If we want young people to be attentive to our teaching, we must be alert to their learning.

P-Persistent: When I've said to others, "Are you a persistent teacher," I often get, "What does that mean?" Simply put: are you supportive of all students? Are you willing to challenge them to be better? Are you sticking with them, even when they might hope you don't? There are many times when letting kids falter may seem impossible to fix. I know; I've felt that. But I've also seen the vast benefit of showing students that we won't let them fall through the cracks when trouble arises in the classroom or social situations. Helping students learn and grow isn't easy, especially when the path is challenging. But it is possible and essential. Persistence may disguise itself as nagging. (It has for me on plenty of occasions.) Don't worry; your ability to be persistent by never giving up on students can make the difference between success and failure.

P-Praise: Every educator I've met believes meaningful praise is precise and valuable. At the same time, there is nothing inherently wrong with saying, "Good job!" It's how often we use praise that matters. If possible, try to use more descriptive actions and words. I'm not suggesting that every bit of praise needs to be lengthy. My point is that praise is part of the human psyche. Some may say that too much praise is overkill, but I disagree. Authentic praise is rarely done for the sake of doing it. Instead, it's providing affirmations when speaking to students that matters. They must know that you mean what you say. Besides being a cornerstone of instruction, recognition or praise will help students feel welcome and appreciated in your class.

Y-Yes: This is my favorite letter of the HAPPY acronym. Many students I've taught feel the same way. Do your students think they can make suggestions for a lesson? How about some of the guidelines for class? More often than we imagine, students want to explore how they learn, get up and move, ask for an extended time, etc. I frequently hear students say, "I won't say anything because it's embarrassing, or the teacher will just say 'no,'" or "I'm just not comfortable enough in class."

To be clear, I couldn't imagine asking for much of anything as a student except the daily, mundane, "Can I go to the bathroom?" While I can't remember every reason this was the case, I know part of it was my teachers were looking for compliance and rarely questions.

Sure, we might be scared of giving up power, uncomfortable taking a risk, or just not seeing the point. Yet, saying **"yes"** and using a student suggestion empowers the class. It shows a higher degree of flexibility and a willingness to adjust for the benefit of learning. I've received many great ideas from students because they felt vested in making the class fun and exciting. Saying **"yes"** shows students that the classroom is about them.

Effective teaching combines many skills and abilities. Sure, it's much more than just the elements of the "happy" acronym I've listed, but those facets are a good start for promoting student engagement and a positive classroom climate.

———

A letter from Kevin:

Mr. Shapiro is the most positive person I have ever met. Every day, no matter what was going on in his life, he would come in happy and smiling from ear to ear to greet his students. Having him as a teacher was the highlight of my sophomore year. His class got me through the day. Going into my sophomore year, I had always heard great things about Mr. Shapiro, but you have to have him as a teacher even to get a glimpse of how amazing he is. Mr. Shapiro goes the extra mile to get to know his students and make the classroom a fun and friendly place. Mr. Shapiro was more than just our teacher; he was our friend.

Mr. Shapiro is the most inspirational teacher I have ever had. His healthy habits and attitude inspired me to eat healthier and get into shape. Mr. Shapiro also inspired me to be more positive and even taught me to be more successful. He taught me to deal with stress and not sweat the small stuff. He taught me the S.M.A.R.T. model I now use to set goals. Mr. Shapiro got me to overcome my most significant problem in school; procrastination. After I had Mr. Shapiro, he made me a better person and helped me dream big.

Kevin Doughty

Class of 2019

You can do it:

1. How do you use persistence and praise as part of your daily teaching?
2. What strategies help you ensure students are attentive during challenging lessons?

Get going:

1. After an instructional unit, use the "H" or another letter from HAPPY in framing questions about what students have learned.
2. After sharing the HAPPY acronym with students, have students devise from each letter their meaning to signify academics or personal attributes.

•CHAPTER 3•
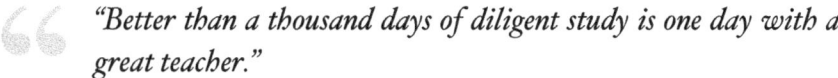
A GREAT TEACHER

> *"Better than a thousand days of diligent study is one day with a great teacher."*
>
> —Japanese Proverb

What makes a great teacher? That's hard to define, but ask many students, and they'll know the answers immediately. They'd say, "A great teacher is enthusiastic, kind, compassionate, funny, organized, passionate, and real!" And that's just for starters. While it's true that many people reading this book will bring experiences and memories to answer that question, even most veterans know that words only touch the surface of what outstanding educators do daily. Teaching is far more complicated than simply walking into a class and being there. Even though many people have opinions on education, those in the field understand the dedication, stamina, and energy required to bring your best daily.

Because of America's educational calendar, we get to start over in a far different way than those in other jobs. We also have an immediate and long-term positive impact on the kids we teach. Such a profound influence should provide newness, energy, and inspiration to our daily approach. These five qualities might be helpful for those who seek some guidance and a little inspiration.

1. **Demonstrate a love for kids.** No matter your role in the
   school, it's hard to reach most students without a particular
   love of helping children and teens. Displaying enjoyment of
   being around students plays a significant role in their success.
   If you like your students, you're off to a great start.

2. **Master your craft.** Be prepared, willing to learn, and
   thoroughly educated in your content area. Your job is to master
   your craft. We can and should always learn more, just as we'd
   expect of our students. You can be an expert in your field now,
   yet losing that edge is easy without continual learning. Being
   engaging, passionate, and determined is a significant first step
   to success.

3. **Meet kids at their level.** No matter what college you
   graduated from, or the knowledge you command, great
   teachers will find ways to assess what their students do and
   don't understand. Great teachers have learned to grasp when to
   slow down and recognize when comprehension/mastery occurs.
   In a later chapter, "Dad, We're Going Fishing," there is the true
   story of how that works. As a personal example, the first time I
   taught nutrition to my tenth-grade students and realized that
   some couldn't multiply 6 x 9 in their heads, it opened my eyes
   to what I thought they should know and what they did. Gaps

in students' learning must be bridged for the content to have any meaning, even if you thought that knowledge should have already been acquired. We can argue, complain, or blame others for lack of preparation or even students' ability, but our goal should be to meet every child where they are.

4. **Promote a "Can-Do" Attitude.** Please consider that teaching to the top isn't about the smartest kid (whatever that means). Instead, it's challenging and inspiring students in the best sort of way. Excellence in education isn't, nor should it be, every student receiving an "A." Students will always have different strengths and abilities. It's our responsibility to find the best methods for students to excel while also helping them to believe they can succeed. This comes from encouragement and the belief that they "can do" great things. Focusing on giving everyone a fair chance creates higher levels of engagement and encourages everyone to strive for their fullest potential.

5. **Make a connection.** As a big fan of Led Zeppelin, I occasionally played a Zeppelin song to see if any students knew the band. On one particular day, Johnny, a student in my health class, wore a black Led Zeppelin shirt. I complimented his excellent taste. Johnny said, "Yea, Mr. Shapiro, my dad is always listening to Led Zeppelin and classic rock." That one connected moment forged a great teacher/student bond. We never know precisely what may build a connection, only that it happens. The majority of students want to find their place in your class. I'm not sure exactly why Johnny wore the Led Zeppelin shirt, but no matter the reason, we still had that connection because of it. Not everything you do will work, but continually trying will pay off.

6. **Find the most important word that will be your daily goal.** Okay, there are plenty of excellent words that inspire great teachers. The following few chapters focus on the 3Ps and 3Es. As important as they are, I've found the power of

connecting myself to a simple word that motivates me daily. "For me, it's POSITIVE." Naturally, I want to continue working on other attributes as I grow, but being positive is a crucial trait I hold dear and take pride in.

It's impossible to encompass all that it takes to become a great teacher in a few pages. After thirty-plus years, I'm still trying to figure things out. However, that's part of what makes our profession so incredible. Becoming great at any role in education is like riding a bike. You might be scared of falling, getting a flat tire, or bruising your ego, but you keep improving to go further each day. Remember, there will be lots of support to keep you going. Be sure not to stress about those things that don't work. Instead, embrace your amazingness and take pride in all you do for kids. Teaching isn't glamorous, even though it's portrayed as such in many movies and TV shows. But it is one of the most rewarding careers in the world. Never forget the impact you have on children every day.

You can do it:

1. What teacher inspired you to get involved in the teaching profession? How did that person motivate you to become a great educator?
2. Which of the five qualities seems the most natural to you? Which may be the most intimidating? Why do you think that is the case?

Get going:

1. Discover your most important word and why it will help you to become a great teacher.
2. Have students discuss their most important word. They can write it on the board, in a notebook, on a post-it note, or even store it on their phone as a reminder.

• CHAPTER 4 •
≥ The 3 P's ≤

> "The key to effective teaching is to remember how you learned."
>
> — Clive James

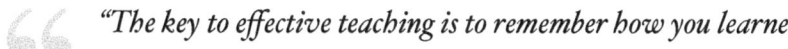

L et me challenge you to take a second and think about the educators who positively impacted your life. Have you considered the qualities that gave them that "wow" factor? You might remember them for their humor, rigor, organization, dedication, or even attention to detail. All of those teachers had certain traits that made them unique. This line of thinking helped me to create the three P's and three E's, characteristics of excellent teachers. They are **Passionate, Patient, Persistent, Empowering, Empathetic,** and **Enthusiastic.** While other aspects make an outstanding educator, hopefully, you'll agree that the three P's and three E's are a great start. This chapter highlights the *P's*.

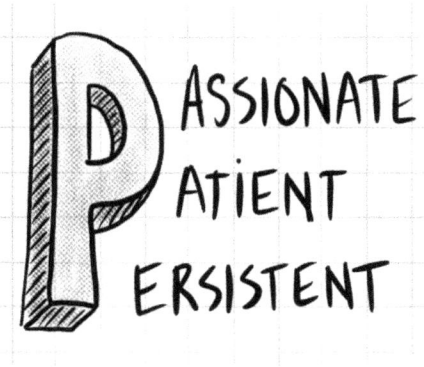

P ASSIONATE
ATIENT
ERSISTENT

1st P: Passionate

Passion is defined as "a strong feeling of enthusiasm or excitement for something."

Being passionate about educating students is an excellent prerequisite for outstanding teaching. It's hard to imagine any excellent teachers who aren't passionate about their work. Passion isn't easy to measure or quantify, but developing dynamic energy is possible with practice and purpose. Having spoken with thousands of kids, I've listened to how important it is for passion to be part of our daily interactions.

My high school Spanish teacher, Mr. Black, was the epitome of "the passionate teacher." His passion for teaching showed in everything he did. When entering the room, he always met students with a smile or greeting. During class, his energy level never dropped. Even when kids, including me, didn't understand the content, he always took the time to address their needs. More importantly, he did it with genuine happiness and kindness. For Mr. Black, showing his passion was never hard!

Another way I recall passion for education was through Mr. Betz, my fifth-grade elementary school teacher, who took pride in how he positively impacted students. Exuding acceptance and kindness to every student, he looked like a hippie from the Rolling Stones era! Even when some of us weren't the best behaved, he offered encouraging words and an enthusiastic pat on the back. On many occasions, he sat down and chatted with me about the positive example he hoped I'd give to my peers. Being a fifth-grade boy, I didn't always apply those principles. However, he never gave up on me and showed his continuous passion for making a difference. Simply put, he made me want to be a better person. Looking back, he was a "game changer" during my earlier younger years of school.

We have challenging jobs that genuinely demand our best each day. Because of those demands, it's easy to see the glass as half empty. However, if we take the approach that students need us at the top of our game—happy, positive, energetic, and excited to teach—we allow passion to become our mantra. That mindset and student-centered thinking will help us even when facing difficult days.

2nd P: Patient

Patience is defined as "to remain calm when dealing with a difficult or annoying situation, task, or person."

In my first year of college, I'll admit that my maturity level was between partying with friends and skipping the 8:00 a.m. class. Luckily, I was fortunate to have Mrs. Gold as my Calculus professor. During one particular bout of immaturity, my friend and I had a laughing fit in her class. Just hearing my friend giggle forced me to start laughing again. Instead of getting upset and being reactive, Mrs. Gold asked us if we were okay and if we needed to go out into the hallway to catch our breath. Even today, I'm still struck by Mrs. Gold's patience and willingness to help us see the bigger picture. Her ability to laugh and stay calm has led me to see the power of showing and modeling patience for students.

Developing patience, like most other teaching habits, is all about practice. There will be instances where your patience will be tested, but teachers who read verbal cues and students' body language can usually nip in a negative situation in the bud. Awareness of smiles, frowns, and conversations as kids enter a room creates a positive atmosphere and allows for addressing students' needs before possible toxic problems occur. Of course, when something does arise, your practice of patience will make those events much less frequent and easier to handle. Here are a few ideas that may help your patience win over students.

Take a deep breath! When you feel frustrated or angry, taking a few seconds to stay calm can do wonders for a situation. Not only can it de-escalate a possible problem, but your ability to show poise also won't be lost on students. They'll admire your patience and may even follow your lead.

Remember, your audience is made up of kids. We are dealing with students. It's unrealistic to think that each one of them will be able to stay calm and composed. Instead of reacting negatively, use phrases and questions that are calming and understanding. For example: "Is there something I can help with?" "Is everything okay?" "Please let me know if you need a second to take a break." These words allow students to realize you're not angry but instead trying to help.

Always remember the end game. We want students to leave with a positive experience. In any complex environment, avoid the escalation of a problem. Some issues are unavoidable. But many times, our actions and words will either win over the students or intensify anger.

Being patient isn't something you can learn in a college class, and it's rarely mentioned during teacher training. That said, it is a trait you can develop over time if you genuinely desire to connect with your students.

3rd P: Persistent

Persistence is defined as "the ability to stick with something."

This final "P" came to me due to numerous coaching experiences and those I've witnessed (see Chapter 11 - POS) early in my career. I was lucky to be surrounded by outstanding coaches who always persisted in being positive and never gave up on their athletes. Initially, I thought this would be an easy task. It wasn't! Getting frustrated when athletes don't follow instructions or understand the key message can sabotage effective learning. The persistent teacher/coach doesn't tell students what to do. They inspire students to be better!

Developing the habit of persistence sounds much easier than it is. As the year progresses, you will have lazy students. This is why being persistent is a requirement. There are various ways to bring persistence into your repertoire. The following are three easy tips to consider.

- Begin early in the year. Make your expectations clear from the beginning. There will be students that test you, and if you're not steadfast with the guidelines for class, you'll just end up changing things frequently and confusing everyone. When I say begin early, I'm simply stating the importance of clearly communicating your high expectations.

- Model the benefits of the great work that students complete on time. Showing excellence from their peers is a way to inspire others to develop or improve their habits. Avoid always picking the same student, but never underestimate the pride factor. When you promote and advertise outstanding achievements from your students (not just those on the honor roll), it has a dramatic carryover influence on other kids in the class.

- Be clear from the beginning that you care about their well-being. I've known persistent teachers who went about this ineffectively. Screaming and punishing a student for not turning in work or being inattentive may seem like persistence. And it is! The message, though, will get lost because of its negative tone. You'll make a tremendous difference when you say, "Listen, I'm sorry for bringing this up frequently, but your success is the most important thing in this class."

As you've read the three P's, consider how being more passionate, patient, and persistent can enhance your teaching and benefit your students

You can do it:

1. Which of these traits do you already exhibit?
2. Which one would be the hardest for you to maintain? Why?

Get going:

1. Ask your students which of the three traits is most important to them.
2. Have students discuss which of the three P's they have.

• CHAPTER 5 •
The 3 E's

> " A genuine leader is not a searcher for consensus but a molder of consensus."
>
> — Martin Luther King, Jr.

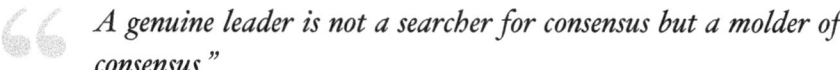

Following the three P's, we move on to the three E's. Again, these three are not all-inclusive. Just as you could find other important " P " words, the same holds for this chapter. I've focused on these words because they also form the backbone of many great teachers.

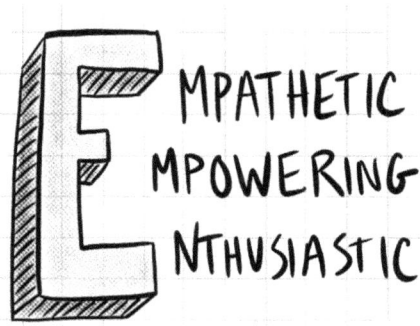

MPATHETIC
MPOWERING
NTHUSIASTIC

1st E: Empathetic

Empathy is defined as " the ability to understand and share the feelings of another."

No matter the grade level, students will experience difficulties in school and their personal lives. Sometimes learning will go smoothly for an extended time, and you'll just sail along, undeniably proud of the progress and fun your students are having. Then suddenly, without warning, showing an empathetic mindset might become the difference-maker for you and your class. Let me share an example.

My dog Izzy, a sixteen-year-old Golden Retriever, passed away a few years ago. Coming into the school that day was challenging. Because I try to maintain a positive attitude, my class could sense that something was off. After a few minutes, I mentioned my dog's passing and how tough it was to lose a fantastic animal. Students could see that my sorrow wasn't because of them but rather from outside forces. Because our class had been built into a robust and positive community, many students were empathetic to my story. They told their own stories about losing a pet. When a teacher shows empathy, the students will respond in kind. Even though empathy might be more visible in the instances I just mentioned, it isn't a "one-and-done" emotion that just comes and goes as the year passes. We'll need to consistently show how much we care about students' well-being, with the added benefit of students reciprocating. Below are three tips that can help keep us focused on building empathy.

- Remember that students have lives outside of our class. It can be easy to get so wrapped up in our content and teaching that we need to remember the hobbies, family issues, and other daily events our students encounter. Understanding our students' lives is paramount to building the power of empathy in school.
- Model empathy. Encouraging students to think about what empathy looks and feels like creates social and emotional recognition norms. Even though the lens of an empathetic classroom/school is rarely talked about, it is essential for building community. Yes, it can be challenging to share our lives. Start small. Just telling a personal story, giving examples,

or even defining empathy will lead to positive discussions in and out of class.

- Reflection on our practice and our daily interactions can be a powerful driver in how we teach and what students learn. I recall a situation where I heard a boy screaming nearby in a hallway. Wanting to be sure everyone was safe, I did a quick check. Once I got there, it became clear that he was standing next to one of our instructional assistants. Over the next five to ten minutes, I observed how the assistant showed empathy, resolve, and compassion toward this student. Not only that, she demonstrated determination and patience. She adjusted her actions and words each moment to meet this troubled boy's needs. By showing empathy, she not only diffused a volatile situation but also showed the student and me how acts of kindness could make a difference in our lives.

2nd E: Empowering

Empowering is defined as "to make (someone) stronger and more confident, especially in controlling his/her life and claiming his/her rights." (Dictionary.com)

I love that definition! Empowering defines what we want students to be in class, school, and even when they graduate. Great schools cultivate a mindset in their students that focuses on ongoing learning—beyond just the school walls. Empowering students, especially if done consistently, is transformational.

Education has, unfortunately, long valued high-stakes testing and grade point averages over a love of learning. This isn't meant to be negative, just factual. We are used to telling students what to do, how long an assignment should be, how many points it's worth, etc. That focus rarely inspires any student to do more than the minimum required. Fortunately, the following suggestions can guide you in the right direction. They are easy to implement and will allow you to build upon the students' steps as the year progresses.

- Please start slow. When I first began establishing an "empowered classroom," I jumped too quickly into making it work. Huge mistake! Students need time to adjust to this different style of instruction and learning. By easing the class into assignments that are easy to follow, clearly defined, and exciting to work on, you'll save yourself the headaches of late work, the quality of work will be much better, and most importantly, you'll have students who will embrace taking more significant steps next time.
- Explain why empowering them is crucial. Let me share my story. Six years ago, we had just finished a quiz. Students had a few minutes to reflect on what they wanted to accomplish. One student, Brendon Sherwood, whom you'll read about later, mentioned, "I want to be a better person!" That struck me to the core. We'd previously discussed being empowered, but his words and actions helped the class to how we might help make his idea happen. While Brendon knew learning the content was necessary, he understood that his purpose in class and school went far beyond just a test, quiz, or project. Teachers and students who feel empowered create a huge ripple effect on their peers, and I'd go so far as to say the school.
- Have a clear goal in mind. Again, when empowerment became one of my goals for instruction, I gave students too many options. It confused us all, from test dates to project choices and many other things. My point is that while choice is precious, you must have clear and measurable goals. A great analogy is a blueprint for a house. You know the dimensions and rooms, but what you do with the inside is unique for each person. In the case of students, you might say, "Our goal is to create a short video presentation on a topic of your choice. It should be between two to three minutes; list why you chose it,

how it's important to you, and where you'd like it to lead." That's vastly different from saying, "I want you to find a topic that interests you, design a project that shows you understand what you've learned, and present it to the class." That might work after your students have gained experience and confidence. Still, suppose that's the initial step. In that case, you'll constantly be backtracking to explain the finer points, and frustration will diminish the positive results you seek.

Empowering our students isn't just some fun, flashy idea. We must stress and impress upon students the importance of learning because it's exciting. Many of the best projects completed in my classes would never have been attempted if I'd stuck with the traditional teacher-led instruction. While my attempts haven't always been easy or successful, the students benefit far more by exploring different learning avenues than by my presenting them with all the material.

3rd E: Enthusiastic

Enthusiasm is defined "as an intense and eager enjoyment, interest, or approval."

Out of all the P's and E's, enthusiasm is the easiest to understand from both a teacher's and a student's perspective. Teachers with high levels of enthusiasm generally like their jobs, make a difference in students' lives and positively impact the school culture. When you see those teachers in action, it's evident that they enjoy teaching. It's hard to imagine an enthusiastic teacher not having some of the earlier qualities listed. Some traits may be more visible than others, but enthusiasm for teaching and learning is necessary for every class and school. I recommend these tips.

- Others may disagree with this, but acting enthusiastically can help change the temperament of a negative person. Our brains will rewire if we repeat the same actions and attitudes. Plus, in time, others will see your enthusiasm and, in return, show appreciation and happiness because of your enthusiastic nature; it becomes contagious. A happy teacher promotes happy students! It's all about the energy you give off. Your enthusiasm will become part of your daily mantra if you're consistent.

- Stand at the door of your room. While it's not the end all be all, it will promote an enthusiastic classroom. Being at the door quickly generates interaction through "Good morning, hello, how are you, etc." Even your simple acknowledgment of your students will set up the class for a more positive experience.
- Begin each lesson or class with something uplifting. Similar to greeting students at the door, this intentional, initial positive reaction to students will carry into your lesson. Teachers want students to love their class. They want children to come in smiling and feeling a part of a community. Enthusiasm is a great builder of this.

After reading the three P's and three E's, I'm hoping you'll reflect on how important they are for your career in education. As I've highlighted throughout the chapter, each can be developed.

You can do it:

1. Which one of the traits mentioned best represents you?
2. Which of the three traits would be the hardest for you to establish in your class? Why?

Get going:

1. Ask your students which of the three traits in a teacher is most important to them. Discuss why this is so. Then try to work on the skill they mentioned.
2. Ask students to think about or even discuss if they have any or most of the 3Ps and 3Es.

•CHAPTER 6•

RELATIONSHIPS

 No significant learning occurs without a significant relationship."

— Dr. James Comer

I am starting this chapter with a post from my friend and fantastic English teacher, Gwen Thackray. Gwen, thank you so much for sharing such poignant words about how a classroom built on solid relationships is a win-win for everyone.

"Today, I stepped back as a teacher and just listened to my students talking on a Friday afternoon, the last period of the day. I laughed a lot! They most likely thought I was crazy, but when you take a moment to really hear them, it's so worth it. They are funny, random, and human. It's one of the best aspects of working with teenagers. It's times like these when I really love my job!"

The easiest and best way to create a classroom where students want to be is grounded in relationship-building. Below are comments from students about a school built on relationships. These are common themes in any class where relationships are a priority.

- The class always felt welcoming and cheerful.
- My voice was going to be respected and heard.
- A positive vibe carried me through the day when walking into the room.
- The teacher treated us as equals, not only as students.
- Every student was recognized for their strengths.

- The relationship between student/teacher and student/student was based on respect.

Purposeful connections shape students' lives. Students will be influenced much more by a caring atmosphere than by one specific lesson you teach. Content matters; to say otherwise misses one of the critical goals of education. However, do not ignore the strong links between the relationship with your students and the learning environment. Students who feel respected, admired, and part of a welcoming class will want to succeed. Even if we can't control everything in their lives, we can ensure the time they spend with us is meaningful. Let's make sure that happens.

Here are five easy and creative ways to build those connections when the school year begins:

1. **Learn students' names quickly.** You often hear from teachers, "I have so much trouble remembering names." Even though there are many strategies to try, I stick with one that always works, is fun for students, and allows for creativity: the name tag! Having students make name tags on day one shows you want to know who they are and builds a quick connection while also being a stress-free way to start the year. As they make the tags, you can walk around the room and start picking up students' names and discover their creative side.

Additionally, the name tags are an excellent way for the students to interact with new peers. I have had them keep their name tags out for most of the semester, even after learning their names. Another benefit is using name tags for notes and motivational quotes, enhancing discussions, and building classroom culture.

2. Explore cultural differences and build awareness.

Every child is unique. This may seem simplistic on the surface, but making sure to address cultural norms and differences is more critical than ever. The beginning of the year is the perfect time to skim the surface of cultural identities. While some students may be hesitant to share their background or culture, you can model how this might look with some authentic personal stories. Although not every teacher likes to share their life with students, even little things like your favorite music, foods, hobbies, or pictures of your family show a humanistic side that students can follow. If you are a teacher who loves to share and connect with your students, do keep in mind (especially in the beginning) that you should avoid getting overly personal or delving too profoundly by asking intrusive questions. Instead, questions like these are great starters: "What did you do this weekend?" "What was your favorite food that you ate this week?" "What's a hobby you enjoy?" "What's your favorite television show?" Plus, having students jot down their answers on paper and reviewing them later in the year can lead to fun class projects.

3. Find some time each class to speak with *every* student.

The start of the year is a great time to start this practice. Even a 30-second conversation as they enter, leave, or during class can have a meaningful influence on the mood of the classroom. Avoid letting a specific lesson plan get in the way of building those strong bonds with the class. Not starting this practice early will make it much harder for the connections to stick later. Daily interactions not only impact the socialization of the classroom, but they also contribute to academic success.

Besides the benefits of culture building, developing those connections early is an effective way to avoid disruptions later. While you might have behavioral issues in the school year, they will be dramatically reduced and limited in their severity when students know a teacher cares about them.

4. Watch body language when students enter the room.
Science has shown that body language is a significant part of communication. When kids stare at the ground, avoid eye contact, or just seem unhappy, this gives the teacher a perfect opportunity for positive intervention. A hello, smile or brief conversation may improve a mood or provide a chance to discover what's happening. A very interesting mantra I've used for class is, "Smile when you enter and smile when you leave!" It may seem hokey, but smiling frequently is a mood enhancer. Also, being aware of common body language signs can help you address possible situations where an intervention is necessary.

5. Create a place of respect, creativity, and caring. Each of our classes is a small community of different young people. Just as our environment shapes us, so does the space we create when students enter our classroom. Students feel part of a family when our class is built around trust, respect, honesty, communication, and dignity. That might seem like a stretch, but think about the atmosphere of your favorite classes when you were a student. They were places where you felt connected to others, including the teacher. Feeling safe and supported without being judged was the norm, not the exception. Conversations were encouraged. We were made to feel special in our unique ways. In short, they were places you *wanted* to be instead of had to be! Creating this kind of class is totally under our control. From setting up the room with pictures and quotes on the wall; to playing music and genuinely promoting a comfortable space, we can directly influence how students feel in our class.

I've decided to finish this chapter with a letter from Brendon Sherwood, a member of my tenth-grade health class, in 2014. I chose his letter because I remembered when he said, "I want to be a better person!" That profoundly impacted how I thought and still think about each lesson in class. Brendon's words helped me realize our immense responsibility towards our students.

––––––

Brendon's Letter

"In elementary, middle, and high school, you take countless classes. It's no wonder, along the way, you are bound to forget many of them. However, Mr. Shapiro's class was one that I will always hold on to. Early in the semester, Mr. Shapiro asked the class to write something they would like to learn on a notecard this semester. I wrote, "how to be a better person." I wanted to learn life skills I could take with my everyday life. I wanted to know more about right from wrong, how to improve another person's day, and how as an individual, I can make the place I live in—simply better. It is safe to say I learned more about myself in that class alone than in any other class in my school career. Throughout the semester, we discussed what healthy relationships consist of, not taking everyday things for

granted, improving ourselves as a whole, and being a better person daily. These were some of the many values that I have kept with me even up to today.

I vividly remember a discussion in Mr. Shapiro's class in which he was describing his trip to a country outside of the US. It resonated with me profoundly because we discussed how incredibly fortunate we are to have what we have every day. I remember that discussion hitting me hard because I imagined going home without heat, running water, or a light to turn on at the tip of my finger. There are countless things I learned in Mr. Shapiro's class, things that have humbled me, and things that have helped me keep my chin up and head on straight.

Brendon Sherwood

———

You can do it:

1. How do you or will you foster positive relationships in your class?
2. How do you develop a classroom where all students feel respected, loved, and accepted?
3. Recall a student relationship that demonstrated the importance of building connections. How did that impact some of your future lessons?

Get going:

1. At the beginning of the year, ask students what makes them unique and how they can make the class an excellent place for each other.
2. Have students work in groups to develop their list of how to build strong relationships in class. Share out their lists.

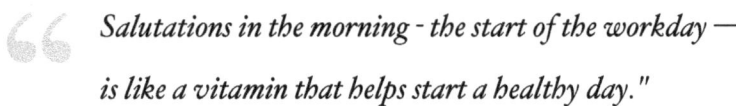

• CHAPTER 7 •
SALUTATIONS · 101

> *Salutations in the morning - the start of the workday —*
>
> *is like a vitamin that helps start a healthy day."*
>
> — Steve Catigan

W e are creatures of habit, just like our students. Each of us has daily rituals that get our day going, hopefully in a positive manner. While there are no magic bullets for everyone, using "salutations" has always been one go-to I've used throughout my career and still do today. Being a greeter for students is a no-brainer. Even though it's not done with a specific motive, those kind words or gestures have benefits that go far beyond "hello" or "good morning." Positive interactions occur even when "teaching" isn't happening.

About five years ago, I had a first-period prep. Next to my classroom, another teacher, the fabulous Mrs. Reach, was preparing for her class to begin. I decided to peek in and say "good morning" to her and the students. I'd done this before, but on this particular day, the results gave me some pause on the power of salutations. "Good morning, everyone!" As I waited for a response, Mrs. Reach said, "Good morning, Shappie!" While I didn't expect all students to respond, I was surprised that other than Mrs. Reach, only a few students took the time to say anything in return. Instead of giving up, I repeated, "Good morning," and most students replied. With the above thoughts spinning in my brain, I decided to follow up with my class. Of the 25 students, 21 greeted me, two gave me a high five, and the last two did nothing. Next was step number two of the experiment. When the students were seated, I gave each one a blank piece of paper. I silently counted how many students said, "Thank you." I said to each student who did, "You're welcome." Returning to the front of the class, I said loudly, "Eleven." Many students looked at me cluelessly. Once again, I said, "Eleven." After a few more blank stares, one of the girls said, "I got it. That's how many students responded with "Thank you." Salutations are all about relationships and building positive habits.

The dynamics of a room that starts with greetings, happy interactions, and anything that raises the positivity bar is easy to see. The best part is how these meaningful interactions can occur, whether as part of a planned lesson or as a random occurrence. We are role models. Even if we don't think it is part of our job, the responsibility is forced upon us because of daily time commitments with students. Saying "Good morning, "Please," "Thank you," and "You're welcome" to students is one of the best ways to model a civilized society and build those initial connections. Getting into the habit of using daily salutations takes persistence. Here are two simple suggestions that can surprisingly impact students' manners and behavior in class.

Signs: Place signs outside your door that speak to entering with a smile or have a motivational quote. Creating this entrance will help students remember that you hope they come into the classroom with a pleasant and respectful demeanor. You can even stand outside the door, a much better option, to remind them to check out the signs, especially early in the year when they might not even notice they are there. Another idea that will impact many students and even staff is from my good friend and fantastic leader, Christopher Jones (@drcsjones) - author of *Seeing To LEAD* (great book).

Chris and I were doing a podcast together, and he mentioned this fabulous idea. His school calls it, #WelcomeSignWednesday! He does different quotes and has faculty and students join him each week. I love how Chris uses different phrases to convey a message of inclusion, community building, and shared culture. There is even a picture with words in Portuguese, that stands for "start your day with a smile."

Hands: Greeting with a handshake or high five can be impactful as students enter or leave your room. The positivity of the human touch with students of all ages can be dramatic and lasting if done regularly. Many teens enter and leave my class by either shaking my hand or giving a high five. Sometimes this happens even when they are seated and working on a project. It's funny and catches them off guard, but it always comes with a smile. It also fosters eye contact. (Try shaking hands or high-fiving somebody and staring at the ground. Trust me; I've tried it: I missed one of my student's hands. Very embarrassing!) Once you make this action a habit, students won't let it go, and you'll be doing it for years to come—one quick caveat to handshakes and high-fives. Please read the body language. Some students may feel uncomfortable with touching, so it's best not to force the issue.

Sometimes the most straightforward actions or rituals are the most effective and easiest to accomplish. My experience watching many other excellent teachers shows that consistently starting each day with a cheerful salutation makes a positive difference for students.

You can do it:

1. In what ways do you use salutations as part of your daily routine?
2. How do students react to the various salutations you use daily?
3. If salutations have yet to be a consistent or deliberate action for you, what might prevent you from trying them?

Get going:

1. At least once a week, greet students at the door as they enter your room. Discuss the positive implications of those behaviors with the class.

2. Create one or more welcome signs outside your room as students enter. You can even have students design their own as the year progresses.

• CHAPTER 8 •
Promises, Promises

 It is easy to make promises—it is hard work to keep them."

— Boris Johnson

I f you're like me, you're in the habit of giving an opening-day speech to students. I've done this for so many years that it's just a ritual that gets students thinking positively about our class. While there is always value in these types of beginnings, I believe that sometimes students get immune to these speeches since they are more the norm than the exception. With that said, a few years ago, a game-changing idea came from a student who got me thinking about promises.

After my "opening-game-day" speech regarding class guidelines and expectations, I received a thought-provoking question. "Mr. Shap, what can students expect from *you*?" After sitting there dumbfounded for five to ten seconds, he said, "I'm so sorry, Shap! I didn't mean to be disrespectful." I replied, "No disrespect at all; I'm grateful for your question. Give me a day or two to think about a fitting response."

He made me think about teacher responsibilities in a new light. Many of us who teach give guidelines, expectations, or rules that students must follow. There isn't inherently anything wrong with that. But students should also know what they can expect from us. Simply put, our promises will help model, motivate, and inspire. There is also a human, authentic side when your promises focus on connections. Especially at the beginning of the year, this allows students to see us in a light they might not be aware of yet. Before I make promises to students, I envision essential aspects of the class and whether I'd be able to fulfill my promises consistently.

Eventually, the decision for me came down to these two promises. First, I promised to listen when students spoke. Second, I promised to come to class happy with a positive attitude. In those few instances where something unforeseen happens, or I'm just having a tough day, the students always know why I feel that way. It allows the promises to be kept and models the idea that none of us are perfect.

Ideally, I thought about relationship building, showing a humanistic side, and being authentic. Yours will most likely be different. Keep in mind that the beginning of the year should focus on interpersonal connections, feeling welcome in class, and students wanting to share their voices in a positive, authentic way.

On the other hand, if you make more than one promise, as I did above, you might even focus on the academic piece. Such academic promises might focus on turn-around time for graded work, approaches to assessments, or any other daily educational aspect of your class. Again, I'd only do any of these if you have another promise that builds on forming connections with students.

Generating an essential list of possible ideas can be helpful because it gets you thinking about what promises are vital for you and those you teach. Here are five promises to consider.

1. Reflect on one positive part of the class each day.
2. Get work back to students quickly.
3. Connect with a certain number of students in every class.
4. Greet your students as they enter the room.
5. Call a parent each week with a positive, upbeat message.

Another significant aspect of making your promises is following this up with a student promise from each person. As an opening activity, it immediately gets them thinking about what they can do to improve themselves academically or socially. Plus, if they happen to falter (which they probably will), you can quickly remind them about their promise. Here are some of the great promises that many students have listed:

- Stop procrastinating (always a huge one)
- Come into class smiling
- Be attentive to the teacher and other students
- Avoid being on my phone and focus on my academics
- Do my best to enjoy school

I'm so grateful for the student who made me explore this. It's forced me to remember my goal of making class impactful for kids. Creating a promise to students will get you immediately off to a good start and offers an excellent chance to foster relationships. Finally, it is another skill that, with practice and determination, will transform your space into an environment where students want to learn.

You can do it:

1. What habits or daily promises do you use to keep yourself motivated and excited about teaching?
2. How have you helped your students to develop positive daily habits?

Get going:

1. Pick one promise to students that you can keep for at least a month. Make it specific and share it with students so they know your goal.
2. Ask students to make and keep a school-related promise for at least a week. Follow up on this after the week with a discussion about how this helped them in school.

• CHAPTER 9 •
AIM HIGH

> *Perfection is not attainable, but if we chase perfection, we can achieve excellence."*
>
> — Vince Lombardi

After a few years of teaching at Washington Elementary in Camden, New Jersey, I'd gotten to know many teachers at school. I recall frequent instances where we'd have conversations about how when you told people you taught in Camden, they'd either say, "Wow, that must be tough," and give you a look or kind of smile in a "Glad I don't have to be at that school." Most of the time, we'd say, "It's sad that people don't know what's happening in our school. These kids are great."

I can't know why most of us felt that way but believing that students can succeed significantly contributed to their success and ours. Much of that mindset was instilled by our principal, Mr. Kozieja. He spelled out that we must have high expectations for **every** student. His philosophy was that this wasn't an option but a requirement. He said, "Craig, I don't care what a student's background or situation is; it's your job to expect and promote excellence. Too often, it becomes easy for others to think that it's acceptable for these kids to do nothing because of where we teach. We can't ever do that."

No matter the students you have in your class, they will see benefits when you provide clear, positive, and sincere high expectations. Along with those expectations, we should avoid toxic talk from others. Phases like those listed below won't promote academic achievement.

- These kids can't do this.
- The work is too challenging.
- They lack the support system to do great work.

Kids (like most adults) will rise to the level of greatness placed on them. If you expect your students' best, you'll see changes in your class and the school environment, and everyone will benefit. Believing in your students is entirely within your control.

Because of the academic testing craze, it's easy to see why teachers may underestimate their influence on students' learning. That's sad but also a false narrative. We create our class and school. Sure, other people play a significant role in education, but a teacher leads a classroom. Students who understand how strongly you believe in their success are more likely to want to be their best. They feel pride and ownership in their learning. Your high standards also help maintain an orderly classroom where students learn to treat you and their peers respectfully.

For some students, we will need repeated efforts to communicate what excellence looks like. Yes, it will be incredibly frustrating sometimes. You might feel uncomfortable being blunt when telling students exactly what you think. For example, I learned this from one of my students, who I thought could have been more productive in class. After trying gentler methods to motivate him without success, it was time to get straight to the point. When I called him lazy, it wasn't necessarily "nice." However, he understood my expectations. More importantly, he knew I wasn't trying to offend him because of our repeated conversations and positive relationship. Instead, it was about providing him with honest guidance about his capabilities.

You'll, of course, have to build those relationships before being so blunt, and my method may be too harsh for you. But it will take a level of persistence for you and your students since it's so easy just to let things go. Here are three ways to aim high.

1. **Use positive reinforcement.** Ensure your students know that you expect excellent work and an optimistic attitude. Despite the subjectivity about what excellence looks like, I'm convinced that pushing every student to earn an "A" isn't the answer. Instead, consider creating a space that fosters each student's best effort and a positive attitude toward learning. For many students, excellence might be earning the so-called all-important "A grade." Still, for some students, a great start would be just showing up to school consistently. Make a conscious effort to know each student by name and praise every student's efforts. Encouraging and supportive reinforcement is critical.

2. **Encourage every student to participate.** Be consistent in promoting a classroom of "all-inclusive" learners. We want

every student to value education and, more importantly, to contribute positively to society. A ripple effect will occur when you let students know you value and appreciate their interaction. Your encouragement will act as a catalyst for greater involvement. If you start the school year with this kind of upbeat message, you'll quickly observe that the class will avoid domination by only a few voices. Early in my career, I allowed and promoted just a few students to carry the classroom conversation. Even when those teens were creative and authentic with their answers, that practice significantly diminished other students' learning and fostered favoritism. Regardless of your strategy, consistently reinforce the message that you see value in opinions and responses from everyone.

3. **Model what you want from your students**. Showing them examples of excellent work and modeling positive behaviors provide a framework for success. We shouldn't assume that students know what we want. Be explicit. For example:

- When providing a challenging assignment, try to give them a model that you've made, or even better, another student's work as an example. This helps ease the stress of something new while also showing students that it's possible to be challenged correctly. Avoid telling students their work must look like the model you've shown. This diminishes creativity and goes against the idea of teaching individuality.
- Praise and positivity are vital when setting the tone in class or school. If we consistently show students that we value their hard work while also praising their efforts, they will follow our lead.
- Don't ever be afraid to admit you made a mistake. Recognizing our mistakes may teach students that it's okay not to be perfect. In addition, we always want students to feel comfortable asking and answering questions. How we deal with our mishaps will impact those essential learning tools.

- Promote other educators instead of being critical. While it may seem harmless to vent around students, leading with what others do well, not their faults, is imperative. We want students to listen to our best, not the worst.
- Lastly, set high expectations for yourself. I can't tell you the power it exudes when your students and colleagues know you love what you do. Students will be inspired by your passion and will follow your lead.

I'll share one final note on having high expectations. Many students will get off to a good start when the school year begins. They are just getting to know you and the other students. It might become easy to not focus on those high expectations. Don't make that mistake. There isn't any risk in telling students what you expect of them. When they hear the same message throughout the school year, they will never doubt that you care about their success.

———

Letter from Olivia

Thank you so much for always being able to listen to what I have to say and for teaching me so many vital points about nutrition and training. Most importantly, thank you for being a fantastic teacher/mentor. This has helped me to be more open and vocal with what exactly is on my mind, how to ask questions about what foods I'm putting into my body, and to start thinking about how I want to look, which is fantastic! I also appreciate how you're always willing to answer any questions and believe in me when I could hardly believe in myself. I realize your job is to teach students, but you've taught me so much about countless things, which I am incredibly grateful for. You love your job, and it's obvious because you're so good at being a teacher/mentor. Your actions have always shown me that you want me to be better at working out, but more importantly, in life. I promise I will be able to perform multiple perfect push-ups by the end of the year. I'm learning to believe in myself, and your belief in me has gotten me a long way.

I just want to let you know that you're a fantastic teacher, and your teaching has inspired so many other students and me at William Tennent. Thanks to you, I want to become a better me, and you've helped me come a long way with training, eating right, and believing in who I am. I'll miss you next year, Shap!

Gratefully,

Olivia Kaczmarek, Graduate 2021

You can do it:

1. What ideas do you currently use to foster high expectations in the class?
2. How do you create expectations that are challenging yet realistic?
3. Do your expectations change based on the students or classes that you have? If so, why?

Get going:

1. Ask students to explain their expectations for your class and discuss how and why answers might vary from person to person. How might their responses influence your power to promote high standards?
2. Break students into groups and use a think, pair, and share lesson to show them how everyone can be successful, even if their answers are different.

•CHAPTER 10•
"The Everyday List"

> *Great things are done by a series of small things brought together."*
>
> — Vincent Van Gogh

* The Everyday List *

✔ Smile when you enter. Smile when you leave.

✔ Do GREAT work for YOU!

✔ Be an awesome LISTENER.

✔ Ask questions; ask MORE questions.

✔ Timely work, is great work.

✔ Don't sweat the small stuff.

✔ Make the class YOUR class!

A teacher posting rules seems like a rite of passage. They usually include instructions like "be quiet," "respectful," "be on time," and "pay attention." While these ideas might be okay, students have usually heard them, and it's possible to create a better message to promote. Because we want students to think from a deeper perspective, it's reasonable to introduce a special list for you and your class. I use "The Everyday List" posted above to promote this. Feel free to use any or all of these or start from scratch. Just remember that guidelines should help students develop skill sets that work with where they are now and in the future.

Here's a quick reminder as you plan your list. These aren't ever set in stone. Whether you emphasize academics, personal growth, or a combination, please explore options that work best for your class. Here is my "Everyday List:"

Smile when you enter the room, and smile when you leave.

I can't overstate the difference that smiling brings to a room. It can encourage students to be more accepting, ready to learn, and even stay on task. Bringing your smile and encouraging the same of your students creates a welcoming atmosphere. Leaving class with that same attitude is just as important. Smiles are contagious and seep into the hallways in our schools.

Do great work for you.

In this age of high-stakes testing, students are constantly being evaluated and compared to their peers. This trap, what I call "competition fatigue," asserts that each student has to produce work similar to that of another student. Even when the intention is entirely harmless or used for motivation, the added stress can wear on kids, especially high achievers who already feel the pressure to excel. Although using examples of excellent work can provide guidelines and set high expectations, they should not be used as the *only* formula for approval. Great work WILL look different for each student.

Be an awesome listener.

Becoming an excellent listener goes beyond just our classrooms. Modeling how to listen helps students socialize acceptably and become responsible and caring individuals while also reinforcing the importance of patience when others are talking. Please know this listening isn't "just being quiet." (That is more about compliance.) Purposeful listening entails eye contact, facial expressions, and a willingness to respond appropriately at the right time. On certain occasions, I'll be talking to students, and they'll be quiet, but their faces tell me they are someplace else (most definitely not sitting in school). To help them build this conscious-listening habit, you'll have to move around, change your tone, check for understanding, and keep things concise. Excessive talking, even if interesting, will lose kids over time. If you need a time requirement, Raleigh T. Philp's book *Tweens and Teens: A Brain-Compatible Approach in Reaching Middle and High School* recommends 20 minutes as the maximum time for students to maintain learning. I stay closer to the 15-minute mark, but the activity, lesson, grade level, and enthusiasm toward teaching will determine your limit. Teachers can model listening skills by asking for student feedback and allowing for breaks, if necessary. This validates their opinions and proves we can listen and adjust accordingly.

Ask questions; ask more questions.

Teachers should encourage students to ask questions. This may seem overly simplistic, but I'm always amazed at how challenging it is for students to speak up. A great tool is pairing or tripling up students and then developing one to two questions: about what they've learned, something they may not understand, or what might come next. They share their ideas with the class, leading to follow-up questions that may not have even been thought of initially. It also helps students feel connected, allows all of them to be contributors, and avoids too much pressure to have the correct answers. With practice and persistence, your class will be asking questions like crazy.

Timely work is great work.

This was one of seven I considered removing because it doesn't exude positivity. I kept it on the list because many students have trouble prioritizing and completing work on time. Since teaching kids about organization and time management is an important life skill, it is imperative to reinforce this frequently. With all the technology available, teachers can quickly notify students about deadlines and upcoming work. Consistently emphasizing the positive outcomes of timeliness will influence their school work and frequently lead to better academic performance.

Don't sweat the small stuff.

Using the book *Don't Sweat the Small Stuff for Teens* by Richard Carlson; students read aloud a chapter each week that focuses on improving some aspect of their lives. This activity ends up being something that students list as one of their favorite parts of the class. It's surprising since many students don't like standing in front of the class and reading. I'm guessing that the book's messages, which focus on life habits, are encouraging and exciting enough to minimize the stress of reading.

Whether you use the book or develop your ideas, the primary purpose is to help students see life's bigger picture. I'd also add that getting students speaking in front of their peers can improve self-esteem and confidence.

Make the class "your class."

Out of all the concepts I've shared, this seems the hardest for students to understand and apply. On the first day of school, I'll say, "good morning, everyone. Great to see you. Quick question for everyone. Whose class is this?" Every student will initially say, "Your class." I'll follow that answer up with, "There are 30 of you and one of me. How can this be my class?" They look at me confused until I explain that it's their class. Unless students take ownership of their learning, getting them involved by their own choice will be limited. Making the class about students should teach them the value of taking risks. My experience has shown me that this becomes challenging if they don't feel their voice is heard

I've found that "The Everyday List" is an excellent starter for teaching students about skills or attitudes that will benefit them in and out of the class. Each teacher can experiment with ideas that work for them. Of course, feel free to use what I've listed. Whatever you decide, think about the APPLE acronym.

- **A**lways provide feedback.
- **P**atience and Persistence make a difference.
- **P**ositivity is the key.
- **L**et students know you care.
- **E**xcellence is the standard, not the exception.

You can do it:

1. What are the current skills or traits that students know you expect of them when they are in your class?
2. What techniques do you utilize for maximum learning and growth?

Get going:

1. Create your everyday list.
2. Consider having students work in groups to create their lists. Then share!

•CHAPTER 11•
Stairway to Heaven

Music is very spiritual; it can bring people together."

— Edgar Winter

Music is compelling. It can cheer us up, make us cry, lull us to sleep, and urge us to dance. Research indicates that the right music can improve our immune response and affect how quickly wounds heal. Music influences our mood and even the chemicals released from the brain.

Music helps students relax, gives them hope, and influences how they function in their daily lives. I recall a tenth-grade boy telling me, "Music has allowed me to escape from the difficult times I had, helped me gain confidence when nothing else worked and allowed me the freedom of expression." As a true lover of music, having it on when students enter the classroom is a mood booster. During the years I've played music in class, many teens will sing along, tap their fingers, or silently move their bodies when they hear a familiar song.

Music is a part of our lives as adults and the young people we teach. It's diverse, so bridging it into students' lives can be a natural extension of culture building.

Suppose you teach at the middle and secondary levels. In that case, you're fully aware, probably too much, of how students' brains are ping-ponging all over the place. This is simply because of the developmental years of adolescence. However, so many teens are constantly listening to music that having it in class can have a calming influence. Plus, playing music can give ownership to students, especially if you allow them to choose **appropriate** music for class. Elementary school is also a fabulous introduction to music. Younger students will dance. It helps create an exceptional classroom atmosphere.

The music choices you play will be determined by your taste and the level of ownership you are willing to share with students. When I start playing music on the first day, I usually play "Simple Man" by Lynyrd Skynyrd because a few lines resonate with teenagers. After that, we typically discuss the lyrics and the types of music students like. Below are some helpful guidelines.

Make sure there isn't any profanity. Even words that might be considered borderline should be avoided to minimize problems. I once accidentally played my wife's playlist on Spotify during class. Too many "F" bombs and laughter from the class! They said, "Shap, keep that on. Your wife has way better taste than you."

Ask students when and why music should be played. Students and the teacher should always know why they are doing something. The answers help validate why music is essential, and you'll even learn some new things about your students.

Mix up the various genres. Some students might be hesitant to mention what they like, so consider having all students put their names and preferences on a piece of paper. Of course, if you're creative, there are many different ways to get this started. When we begin class, I'll often play a song from another student each day.

Always be aware of the volume. My hearing isn't the greatest (too much Metallica, Disturbed, and Zeppelin, along with old age), but remember other classes around you and that some students might be sensitive to loud music.

Experiment with songs that have specific meanings. There are endless opportunities to play music with lyrics that resonate with you and the students in your class. It is about personal taste, but finding songs with deeper meaning can lead to great discussions and even provide an extra incentive for more reserved students to talk.

Stick with it. It's easy to forget about playing music, especially when we are so busy with many other things. If you have an app like Apple Music, Spotify, Tidal, or any other music source, having it in the background for easy use can enhance the class with just a click of a button.

Solicit feedback. Get feedback about your music every few weeks and welcome students' suggestions. Music is a universal dopamine provider. It gives kids a voice in something that is always positive, shows a human side to the teacher, and is a great transitional tool for starting an academic portion of the class. Even if you start slowly, playing music will likely promote a positive and happy classroom. Give it a try.

You can do it:

1. Do you play music in your class? If yes, how do students respond to it?
2. How can music help students feel more comfortable in class?

Get going:

1. Play one popular song each day for a week as students enter your class. Ask them to describe a few words and what they mean.
2. Give them a chance to pick their songs. Please remind them of profanity and avoidance of derogatory language.

• CHAPTER 12 •

PHONE HOME

*Communication must be HOT. That's **H**onest, **O**pen, and **T**wo-Way."*

— Dan Oswald

I had my first real experience working as a summer camp counselor when I was eighteen. One of our first responsibilities as counselors was to contact the parents of each child. I was terrified! My parents suggested I write a brief script, which was a great idea. Unfortunately, my nerves got to me, leading to a stuttering, babbling, and generally incoherent fifteen seconds before a parent asked if I was okay. All I could say was, "I'm sorry." Luckily, she laughed and said, "I appreciate you calling to connect. I know it's not easy calling somebody out of the blue."

Thirty-four years later, after hundreds of phone calls to parents, it's clear that even a thirty-second phone call can be an unbelievably powerful and effective tool for promoting relationships. If done consistently, parents will appreciate your willingness to connect with them, be thankful for the positive message about their child, and greatly appreciate the time spent sharing ideas for their child's success.

I realize that time is usually a factor in how we can best communicate with families. If calling parents by phone seems too daunting, we can still email or meet in person. While face-to-face meetings are a great way to introduce yourself, meeting all the parents in person might be unreasonable.

For ease of use, sending an email is extremely easy and can be done in a short amount of time. It's also generally available to most people. Emails also allow for sharing attachments, like opening letters and other important information.

For me, though, a personal phone call—even just a message left to parents or a thirty-second conversation—allows for tone and reflection and puts parents at ease. Phoning a parent, especially early in the year, reinforces what students have done well, relays expectations, and nips any discipline issues. I have never spoken to a parent who isn't appreciative that they've been contacted with something positive. While I prefer to focus on upbeat phone calls, parents will be grateful that you have taken the time to explain the situation when a problem arises.

Another great benefit of calling a parent with something positive is the "whisper-down-the-lane effect." Kids will talk. If you call numerous parents, there isn't a doubt that those students will tell their friends that you called. A few years ago, some students thanked me for calling their parents; others even asked me if I would call theirs. Even if the call isn't 100 percent positive, the message that you are serious about helping their child will still get through. Furthermore, calling a parent or meeting them early in the year is a great way to supplement a letter or syllabus that might have been sent home just as the year began.

"Who has the time to call every single parent? We barely have enough time to send an email home." Yep, that can often be true. So here are a few suggestions that may make the process seem less daunting and more achievable.

Be proactive. Once the school year gets going, it's incredibly challenging to call parents regularly. You'll assess students frequently, try different lessons, enter grades, and engage in many other duties or initiatives. While I just mentioned the challenges of calling parents, the first week or month of school or even during an in-service day may be a great time to introduce yourself. Keep the phone calls brief (no more than a few minutes) and focus on a simple welcoming message or a positive statement about the student. You can even have a script written.

Make a limited number of calls at a time. For those who have small classes or have the same type all year, it's much easier to contact 30-40 parents than 300. For teachers with hundreds of students, calling one or two parents every few days is much better than doing nothing. Here are five effective strategies to determine whom to call:

1. Pick popsicle sticks at random.
2. Use a "pay it forward" option.

3. Play a game where the winning team gets a call home.
4. Call when a student does something exemplary.
5. Make it a quick surprise to keep kids on their toes.

Start every message, despite its theme, with a positive tone.
I've found this tip the most important of all. It's common sense to begin a conversation with something positive. Yes, some situations are almost impossible, but I encourage you to try a non-confrontational tone. If this seems challenging, take a few minutes before that call and find one thing to start the conversation on a good note. No matter why we contact a parent, our ultimate goal is either helping to fix a problem or acknowledging the great work that their child has done. Putting a parent on the defensive should be avoided.

Remember that meeting parents in person is still the best way to share a positive message. On the other hand, if you start slowly and are persistent early in the year, you'll love the feedback and support you'll get from using your voice.

You can do it:

1. What is your most common method for contacting parents? If you could improve upon that method, how might that be accomplished?
2. How many positive phone calls do you make during the year? What is the general response to that type of phone call?

Get going:

1. Call at least one parent a day for a week and mention the positive traits of their child.
2. Take a few moments and speak to students privately about the impact those positive phone calls have made.

•CHAPTER 13•

PAY IT FORWARD

 If we all do random acts of kindness daily, we might just set the world in the right direction."

— Michael Kornfeld

T hink about your class, school, and even our society. When students leave our class for the day, and eventually the year, what do we hope were the main lessons? Is it the content we taught? The relationships built? The life lessons that may help them in the future? Hopefully, all of them! Sure, academic growth is essential. But we can't deny that students need more than just what's measured by their GPA. Colleges, the military, trade schools, and businesses are looking for skills like communication, problem-solving, risk-taking, initiative, and qualities that aren't always easily measured. That's where paying it forward can be meaningful for our classrooms and schools.

Paying it forward is a common term for many of us. It's simply the concept that when a good deed is done, you follow it up with another person. The hope over time is that a web of giving, kindness, and empathy will become intertwined in our schools. Luckily, it's doable with time and practice. Based on your goals, it's easy to adjust plans accordingly. Remember that even the smallest amount of paying it forward can be significant.

While some older students might be aware of the concept of paying it forward, younger ones and even those in high school will benefit from showing examples or having a classroom discussion on what paying it forward looks like. As a big fan of holding doors and daily morning greetings, I mention those as a quick "get us going" idea.

One caveat before I share some thoughts. I repeatedly stress to students that "paying it forward" isn't mandatory or about a grade. My general guidelines for starting are to keep things simple. We want to avoid having too many directions and making it so complex that students have more questions than answers. Below are a few ideas I've used in the past.

- **The trusty post-it note.** I permanently have colored post-it notes on my front desk as students enter the room. They grab a post-it, write down their "pay it forward," and sometimes share it with the class or attach it to their name tag. By the end of the semester, my desk is cluttered with them.
- **Using Google Docs.** Another easy and very effective way to monitor progress and stay organized is using a Google doc for all your entries. The nice thing about Google docs is how easily you can add comments on their success.
- **Class competition.** While I haven't done it recently, I did spend a few years having classes compete against each other. It was fun, students got engaged, and the winning class had a party at the end of the semester. Some might feel that rewarding a class is too much, yet it's another idea to consider.

Keep in mind that the number of entries will vary significantly among students. This will happen no matter how hard you try to get everyone involved. I've had students with one entry and others with fifty. Please don't force this on students. We should never criticize those that don't get involved. It's the process of getting them to think that is so important.

Another example that is a creative play on paying it forward is called a "Create-What-You-Need Board." A colleague and friend, Teneisha Reach, does this activity; her board is incredible. She also has a distinctive way of getting students to buy into her idea. This student-created bulletin board is where students give helpful tips or motivational quotes to others who might be having difficulty. You can use index cards, post-it notes, or any other technique that works for your class. A student who takes a card is responsible for replacing that card with their helpful idea. I have a picture of mine below.

Here is a quick pay-it-forward through apples story. I would take my children, Alana and Cole, to school each morning. Like other working parents, this has its challenges. Because I was often in a rush, I'd throw an apple or two in my bag as a snack. Because of the hectic pace of getting to school I'd often forget the apples were in my bag. Hence, ending up with twelve apples in my bag! One day, Costco had a great deal on Honeycrisp apples (my favorite), so I bought about fifteen. Then a lightbulb went off. Instead of putting one or two in a bag, I took all of them to school, thinking they should last a week or two. I placed the container in the back of my room, not thinking students might want apples, even though I'm always promoting snacking during class to keep students' energy levels up. I'd eat three to four apples weekly, but the rest would disappear quickly. One day, when I got to school, I went to the back of my room and noticed a large bag of Honeycrisp apples sitting on the counter. The note attached said,

"Shap, thanks for always bringing in apples; I figured you could use a bag for yourself." What a fantastic feeling. Even though we'd emphasized paying it forward, it never crossed my mind that kids would pay it forward to their teacher. I called the student's parents during the class and thanked the student in front of everyone. Not only was the student appreciative, but the message to other students was also evident. Paying it forward pays off!

You can do it:

1. How do you encourage your students to make a difference for others?
2. Why is giving so crucial for children and teens to learn about?

Get going:

1. Craft a Pay it Forward activity for a week.
2. Reflect with your students on its benefits or challenges.

CHAPTER 14

POS

> *Nothing will shape your classroom and school more than being positive around students."*

A s much as I enjoyed teaching at the elementary level, the late dismissal time made it virtually impossible to coach. Yet given my background in exercise, coaching had always been one of my goals. Fortunately, my new job at William Tennent High School had an opening for the head girls' cross-country coaching position. As luck would have it (although it didn't seem like it then), it gave me some true insight into the power of positivity.

Our team was relatively small, and I knew very little about our opposing teams since I was new to the program. Our first scrimmage was against Hatboro Horsham High School. I read about their accomplishments. I quickly learned that their coach, Jen, played a significant role in their achievements Her contagious positivity led to remarkable success with her athletes.

As our first race unfolded, it became clear that Hatboro was no joke. A severe butt kicking occurred. After the meet, being relatively immature, I sulked past her athletes, chatting on top of our hill. Just in passing, I heard them mention how unique *POS* was and how much they felt inspired to run.

During another scrimmage (another butt-kicking, but at least closer), I walked past her girls sitting on our hill again the following year. Feeling more upbeat about our performance, I heard the same word (*POS*) repeatedly spoken by each of the girls. I found Jen and said, "Jen, this is the second year in a row that I've heard girls on your team say '*POS*.'

What does that mean?" Blushing, she said, "It's short for Positive; that's their nickname for me." I wasn't surprised. Jen's positivity confirmed my belief that having a "positive" attitude in and out of school makes a difference.

On many occasions, my children have mentioned the attitudes and behaviors they observe in their teachers. They usually speak about how positive, friendly, and happy teachers make the day go much faster. Hearing and seeing the different moods based on their classes and teachers has influenced my teaching more than they know. A teacher's positivity factor significantly affects how students feel about school. Staff who exude a positive attitude will help students in ways beyond just their class. Positivity is a culture creator. We can have organizational skills and content knowledge and even be creative at assessing students. Still, students won't feel fully vested in our class if our attitude seems negative or unhappy. They might do the work for a grade and their parents, but the class will lack an atmosphere of inspiration that leads students to feel a sense of ownership in their learning.

Some might be wondering why to dedicate a chapter to being positive. Simply put, being positive is possible for just about everyone. It's a mood booster, learning promoter, and social connector that will impact the classroom and school just by its presence. While I can't say it's possible to transform an attitude, working on being positive at the beginning of the year will impact students and faculty. Of course, we can't forget that bringing a happy, inspiring message to students will reduce discipline issues commonly occurring in disconnected classes.

Having an environment that students want to be part of isn't just about the teacher; it's also about their peers in the class. No matter the grade, your class will frequently follow a friend or the socio-center (the student who garners respect and, hopefully, not the class clown). This makes the impact of a positive environment on the class even more important. An aura of upbeat energy will lead to a more engaged, empowered, and less stressful learning environment. Bringing that energy to the classroom can be developed with a plan that's realistic to establish.

Each teacher can find positive activities that will engage their students. With that in mind, I wanted to share my favorite. **It's called "POS." Passionate, Outstanding, and Successful!**

As a big fan of vocabulary words, I wanted to combine a new word and something positive that resonated with the class. POS is it. (It's amazing how many students will use vocabulary words once you teach them.) Each day on my board (Easel of Excellence), I post a word or phrase we cover in class. For example, the opening words in 2021 were *inspirational, unique, trust, smile, expectations, and impactful.* Students would describe them quickly on a post-it note, and we'd briefly chat about what each word meant and how repeatedly using these words could impact their lives. Yes, it might seem like a small activity, but that's the point. Doing these small "things" consistently promotes a strong class community.

Even those students who may not seem like they need it will flourish with a teacher who always brings a positive message to the class. With a consistent effort, any person can make their class or school change for the better. All it takes is a little POS! As evidence of this, I'm sharing a letter from Haley.

————

And everyone kept telling me, "High School will be the best four years of your life, so make them count." Little do they know, students stay up endless hours of the night struggling to do homework, work hard to get good grades, feel pressured into being involved, and try their best to find themselves. Mr. Shapiro has taught me that these trivial endeavors do not matter much in the long run. To this day, he has taught me the most valuable lessons any teacher ever could: "Always stay positive," "Work hard to achieve your goals," "Revel in being kind," and most importantly, "Do not sweat the small stuff." I find hope and strength in Shap's positivity and persistence, even on the worst days. His constant smile immediately assures the people he interacts with that everything will be okay. By doing much more than his job title entails, Shap shapes students' lives to teach them more than just inside the classroom. Mr. Shapiro is tremendously personable and devotes his life to ensuring the students love the person they see in the mirror. I could keep describing the inspiring and encouraging teacher that Mr. Shapiro is, but no words could ever express the magnitude of his influence.

So, as my writing ends, I would like to thank you, Mr. Shapiro. Thank you for inspiring me each day, connecting personally with me and a large portion of William Tennent, and teaching lessons that will be carried with many after high school. Again, thank you for making these four years of high school enjoyable and worthwhile. As a teacher, "you have not only taught me, you have shaped me."

Haley Schubert (2019)

———

You can do it:

1. What steps do you take to be positive each day?
2. How do you overcome those challenging moments or days while still providing hope for your students?

Get going:

1. After spending a few minutes about the impact of positivity in class, ask students to reflect on what they most enjoyed about the lesson and how it impacted their mood.
2. Ask students to think and discuss with their friends how they can be more upbeat about school.

• CHAPTER 15 •

It's all about The Kids

When I think about the last 30-plus years of teaching and coaching, it gives me pause about how many young people I've had contact with—thousands of students. Even though not every moment has been exceptional, I wouldn't change a thing. Whether new to education or veteran, you have a transformative influence on how students function in school. At the age of twenty-three, I didn't comprehend our impact on students, but thirty-four years later, it's crystal clear. We are hopefully in education because we have a passion for learning, a connection with students, a great satisfaction in sharing our knowledge, the opportunity to experience something new every day, and a unique chance to enhance future generations of adults.

Our attitude toward children and teens will directly impact much of what we do in the classroom. When we are passionate about what we're doing and whom we're doing it for, grading papers, designing lessons, calling parents, and the hundreds of other things that often go unnoticed become much more enjoyable. I'd even go so far as to say exciting and rewarding. Realistically, there's no way that I or anyone else can make somebody else love a career. But we can inspire our colleagues to find joy in what we do. If you're in it for the long haul, here are some specific ways to help you make it all about the kids.

Focus on the Good/Great. Even though one of my main goals for the book is to promote a positive lens of education, I'd be foolish to think that cynicism does enter the minds of some. Changes are constantly occurring, and we are often held under a microscope by those who aren't part of education. My best suggestion is to spend more time on all the great things you do daily. That sounds like a pie-in-the-sky remedy, but it works if you practice. Even in those challenging circumstances, maintaining enjoyment will help you remember that it is about the kids you teach.

Enjoy the moments. We meet many outstanding individuals each day. Whether you work in elementary or secondary education, there is never a day when you won't interact with great young people. Plus, many of them are genuinely grateful for the effort we show. Tell your class how much you appreciate all they do each day. I guarantee you'll be amazed at the impact it has.

Appreciate working with others. Education allows us to be more social than many other professions. We should have discussions with our colleagues, without it being a competitive sport. We are personally connected to our peers because our jobs relate specifically to their work. Our collaboration in and out of the classroom greatly contributes to positive discussions and relieves stress when troubles arise. Also, by working with others, we get the benefits of learning new ideas, sharing positive stories, and generally having a chance to vent to receptive ears.

Embrace growth. If you end up staying in education for much of your career, you'll be sure to have many outstanding and even a few challenging years. Unlike many other jobs, we get a SUMMER to reflect and renew. The opportunity for growth and getting a fresh start is always invigorating.

I'm writing this chapter before school ends for the year. I'll miss incredible seniors and my colleagues. However, I'll see other students I've connected with, meet new ones, and still be with amazing co-workers.

Value your impact. Ultimately, we change the world. What we do each day is essential for humanity. Even if we don't realize it, our daily interactions and lessons can profoundly shape how young people see society and their employment paths. If you don't believe this, think about how many careers are based on what a person has learned. Their job choice was likely shaped by a teacher or teachers who positively impacted their lives.

Being in education allows us to build enduring connections with students. We may never know our total impact on their lives, but we must trust that we have positively influenced them. I can't think of a better privilege than being in education. Hopefully, reading this chapter has helped you to identify reasons for enjoying your job and fostering the growth that all students deserve.

You can do it:

1. What is the most rewarding part of your job? Why?
2. How have you impacted students in ways that go beyond just one lesson?

Get going:

1. Pick a few days in the beginning, middle, and end of the year, and write down how your students have positively impacted you.
2. During one or more of those times, please tell students how much you enjoy being their teacher.

Notes

Section Two

When the Rubber Meets the Road

My family was recently out to dinner chatting about my son's upcoming graduation from high school. We were reminiscing about those teachers who'd impacted him in meaningful ways. It led to our frequent (annoying, as my kids would say) conversation about how poor of a student I was in high school. I'd ramble on about how we didn't have the technology or all the different ways to access information that current students have. Even if my son didn't get exactly where I was coming from, I know that for me, my brain and sitting all day just didn't cut it. Just as important was that most of my teachers didn't step out of their comfort zone to make learning exciting and engaging. The few that I did have, Mr. Black in high school and Mrs. Gold in college, showed me what excellence in teaching could look and feel like.

Before I get bashed for blaming the teachers for my laziness, I need to clarify that their styles might have worked great for other students but not for me. That's a critical point that I hope resonates in this section. No matter how engaging, creative, and authentic your instruction might be, it's imperative to self-assess our teaching. Also, it's impossible to reach every student precisely the same way. I had a student a few years ago say, "Mr. Shapiro, I don't like your class; you're too positive for me!"

At the heart of our daily lessons is a combination of the Art and Science of teaching. For example, I can't count the number of times I've told students the 4-4-9 rule of carbs, protein, and fats. There is a certain level of confidence that students will remember those numbers because they've been repeated many times. That is the science of repetition. But without some kind of connection, those numbers mean very little.

On the other hand, if I bring in an "apple" and explain/show that the apple has 80 calories and 20 grams of carbs, students can see, hear, relate, and even taste the lesson. That is the Art of Teaching. Both matter, but how we blend them will ultimately drive the success of your class and the learning that occurs.

This section of the book connects those ideas to create an atmosphere I call "The Positivity of Learning." This doesn't mean every moment or day is filled with Kumbaya lessons. Instead, the way we blend things makes the class special. The main concepts in this section focus on how teaching, assessing, and general practices can be more enjoyable and meaningful. As I've mentioned, I'd love for you to share what's been working for you even when you've hit a roadblock.

• CHAPTER 16 •

I am Still a Teacher Because...

I am still a teacher because of the extraordinary amount of unity and teamwork that goes into making our schools unforgettable. In one of our recent school-wide events, Black and White Night, students were involved in athletic and academic competitions. I was running around judging and watching various activities on one particular gym night. As teens danced and played an intense game of speed pyramids, I watched parents, fellow teachers, and hundreds of students cheering. Besides the energy in the air, it helped me see the true power that can occur when we bring together families, students, and faculty.

Driving home at 11:00 p.m., exhausted, I reflected on why I am *still* a teacher today. I love my job just as much now, even though it began over thirty years ago. Besides my example above, here are more reasons that may resonate with you. Hopefully, you'll share some of your reasons.

 I am still a teacher because meeting hundreds of students each year is inspiring. Even though learning all those names can be challenging, the reward is worth it. Seeing how motivated young people are about wellness makes coming to work each day exciting.

💜 **I am still a teacher because** students feed off our positivity. A certain aura of energy happens when children and teens witness a teacher's enthusiasm.

🤍 **I am still a teacher because** even when challenging moments occur (and they will), amazing colleagues encourage me to focus on being happy and leading by example.

💜 **I am still a teacher because** students know when someone truly cares about their well-being. While our daily interactions and attitudes may seem small, they transform lives.

😆 **I am still a teacher because** few other professions offer the opportunity to make such a profound difference to an entire generation.

😋 **I am still a teacher because** there is never a dull moment. No matter your role in education, there will never be a lack of excitement.

📖 **I am still a teacher because** as much as education has changed over time, the core values will always exist.

😇 Finally, **I am still a teacher because** there has never been a time when teaching young children, kids, and teens was as important as now.

Please consider your why in the context of your impact on schools and classrooms. You can still be excited about summers off, a regular paycheck, and other teaching perks. But none of those things will keep you in the field for decades if you don't like being around kids. Whatever motivates you about being in education, "I am *still* a teacher because" is grounded in making a difference for students, colleagues, and communities.

You can do it:

1. What is your "why I am still a teacher?" What positive ideas could shape your career if you're just starting or finishing college?
2. How will your "why" promote positive growth and learning for students?

Get going:

1. Pick one goal to keep your "I am *still* a teacher because" going into the future.
2. Write about how that goal inspires you to be better each day.

• CHAPTER 17 •

Thanks, Ed! This 'P' is for You!

 Sometimes our conversations with students genuinely change our world!

Embrace them, learn from them, and enjoy them!"

O ne of the joys of teaching older students comes when they are about to graduate from high school. We see the culmination of work, friendships, sports, activities, and growth of a young teen to a budding adult. Frequently, we sign yearbooks to remember the time spent together. Eddie, thanks for making this chapter essential to being "purposeful."

I'd never had Eddie as a student. Still, I was fortunate to have built a solid relationship after school and during some of our exercise sessions. Before graduation, we'd spoken about getting a yearbook signature. At about noon, Eddie entered my room with a yearbook in hand.

As I look fondly back on our conversation, Eddie and I came up with keywords mentioned in our long time together: *kind, sincere, generous, and determined.* I'm not surprised since Eddie has all of them! But one other word stuck with me on that day, as it still does today: *purposeful!* After almost two hours of talking, we finally ended with a genuine handshake and smile. I want to thank Eddie for inspiring me with this chapter, and I hope he will read it one day.

From the time we enter our buildings to the time we exit them, purposeful actions, words, and behaviors impact the lives of others for the better or even worse. Take a moment and think about the following ten steps:

1. Shaking hands/high fives and saying "good morning" as students enter the room.
2. Telling a personal story that connects with students.
3. Dressing in a unique costume to emphasize a particular lesson.
4. Getting kids moving at just the right time.
5. Walking around the room as groups are working.
6. Using words that praise and connect with students.
7. Bringing in a healthy snack after your students have worked hard.
8. Calling a parent with a positive message.
9. Forgoing a quiz if the students aren't ready.
10. Doing a cultural get-to-know-you activity.

Each action is done in conjunction with a "purposeful" idea. More importantly, they contribute to improved learning and a great class-room environment. At its core, being purposeful is about intentionality. How we develop these skills, talents, and actions depends on each teacher's style. That said, specific strategies can help foster purposeful teaching.

Start Small - "Throwing a surprise party" is an example of a purposeful action that can make a big difference for your class. Some might find this extreme, but instead of making it an all-out bonanza, you could just have some snacks, play music, and celebrate success in class. Find some way to let your students know you appreciate their efforts and making progress.

Use Proximity - In "10,000 Steps," which is about the importance of movement (see chapter 23), I explain the value of proximity and activity in class. Being an active agent in student learning is one purposeful choice any educator can make as part of their daily teaching.

Chat with Them - In my discussion with Eddie, the word *purposeful* only emerged because we were having a real-life conversation. Speaking with your students about their lives is a great way to see who they are and what's important to them. By actively listening and engaging in conversations, we can frame lessons around meaningful dialogue that will inspire them.

Use Brain Breaks - Brain breaks aren't just a catchy term. They are grounded in common sense and research. Our brains need small doses of learning, which allow our brains to reset. They also improve socialization and reduce learning intensity (look at kids' faces during tests). There are no exact rules for this strategy because every teacher needs to find a balance. I've witnessed teachers use short breaks approximately every 15-20 minutes.

On the other hand, a teacher could use a combination of time and the "yawn" factor. You observe students' behaviors, actions, and participation and then make minor adjustments. Your class, the lesson, content, grade level, and other variables will contribute significantly to applying breaks. Just make sure the break is purposeful.

Watch Body Language - Being able to read the room and your students' facial and body language may sound strange. Still, I've found it's one of the best ways of assessing what they know, how they feel, and when you might have to adjust a lesson. A perfect example is when students drop their eyes when they know questions are coming. Sure, some kids are just plain shy. But from personal experience, I've witnessed that more students avoid eye contact when the content is challenging. Knowing this can help alleviate stress and allow you to converse about not being afraid to ask a question or admit you don't know something.

My conversation with Eddie inspired the concept of purposeful teaching. It isn't something that can be accomplished with one great lesson. Developing your unique style will take time, both in the present and future. Don't worry if you happen to stray off course or forget. With lots of purposeful practice, you and your class will reap the benefits.

After graduation, Eddie and I chatted again. At the end of our discussion, I asked him, "So, Eddie, what is the word we'll use going forward to describe how we do things?" He said, "Come on, Shap, it's all about being purposeful!" To confirm this, here are Eddie's thoughts:

———

Shap, you have taught me many things, not as a teacher - as I was never that fortunate - but as a friend. The most fitting way to describe our relationship is to recall our last talk.

As I walked the halls looking for teachers to give my farewell, I remembered you wanted to see my yearbook, which I assumed meant you wanted to sign it or something simple. Well, as we both know, this was more than just the usual yearbook signing between most students and teachers. Nonetheless, I decided to save the best for last, so you were the last person I visited.

Over the hour and a half we spent talking (I know . . . neither of us expected that!), much was discussed. The one word that seemed to stick out from our conversation was "purposeful." As I write this, I can testify that I still keep that word in mind so that I may strive to live my life to the fullest.

Shap, this short story does not serve you justice. For someone to understand who you are, he must meet you. As I and almost everyone else who knows you can confirm, you are a fantastic father, teacher, mentor, and friend. Thanks to you, especially the students from William Tennent High School, countless lives have been impacted. Your optimistic and loving nature are just two characteristics that make up your well-roundedness. For an older man (just kidding), you are in excellent shape. Your active lifestyle has contributed to your solid mental state, which is that of the most accomplished human being.

Shap, you are a fantastic man, and it is an honor to call you my friend.

Love ya, Shap.

Eddie Shead

———

You can do it:

1. How do you incorporate purposeful activities? What might a few look like?
2. Do you give yourself time to assess if those lessons work as planned?

Get going:

1. Use a purposeful activity from the list above or create your own and reflect on its impact.
2. Have students discuss the importance of being purposeful in their own lives.

• CHAPTER 18 •
Train Your Brain

The baseball swing is a very finely tuned instrument.

It is repetition, more repetition, then a little more after that."

— Reggie Jackson

"Shap, I can't remember these numbers and concepts. We don't do math like this." I said, "It's okay; you must **train your brain** to recognize and remember completely new information. Trust me; it will work." That phrase, "train your brain," became an essential catchphrase for not only those students but also part of an ongoing theme to help kids get connected to information. The great thing about such a phase is that students latch on to it when remembering information, staying positive, breaking a habit, or even improving their wellness. Sometimes students and adults will resist this notion of "training your brain" as too time-demanding, confusing, or tedious. When training your brain started, one of the students sitting upfront mentioned that he couldn't remember anything.

I said, "4682." The class looked at me like it was morse code. I repeated, "4682." We discussed that if you don't repeat the number and connect it to something, your brain will quickly forget it. Every few minutes, I'd say, "number, please." The students would say, "4682" Even for this simple exercise with a meaningless number, students needed practice to recall it. Now, imagine how much repetition is necessary for students to understand or master a complex concept for which they have no background knowledge.

Throughout our lives, we remember many concepts because of the time spent working on them. This was true for me in learning how to ride a bike and memorizing the times tables. While I don't ride quite as often or multiply as I did in school, those skills became embedded in me from repeatedly wearing out thousands of erasers and making the Band-Aid company a household name! Teaching and learning is always about helping students by using repeated practice and styles of instruction instead of moving on when they aren't ready. For authentic learning to occur, it's the "Use-it-or-lose-it" principle. Repetition and practice are necessary if our goal is understanding. The ideas presented below can get you on the right track to having students connect with your content.

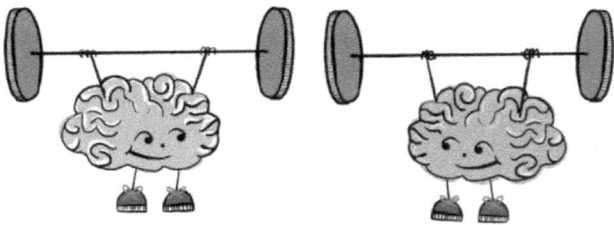

Have students write often. Writing will always be a universal learning skill. Writing is also one of the best ways to see if students truly understand what they've learned. Having words on paper flows across all curricular areas and allows for meaningful feedback. Whether it's through a student's reflection, partner reading, teacher evaluation, or even group work, the practice will pay off. If a student can write well about a topic, it is an excellent gauge for showing that learning may be permanent. Once they write about something, it's great to have them share what they wrote with classmates.

Make them explain, explain, explain. Speaking goes hand in hand with writing. When students articulate the steps to a problem, the plot of a story, the historical context of an event, or other details of lessons, it's not only rewarding for them but also shows they have vested them-selves in their education. It's why the initial start to the year is critical. Getting students comfortable talking leads to greater confidence in taking risks and answering questions. While things are never impos-sible to change, student chatter is much easier to accomplish if done early on. Also, explaining doesn't have to be verbal. A quiet, reserved student can flourish through projects, games, technology, and other tools. This type of teaching can provide alternative activities for students who want to avoid the spotlight.

Keep them on their toes. I previously mentioned students who might stare at their desks for fear of answering questions or being called on. I generally try to nip this in the bud and say it positively: "Eye contact is a great life skill. When your classmates or I'm talking, please be attentive. It also tells us you're ready to answer questions." I won't lie; it's funny when they say, "Huh," or immediately lift their eyes to me when the questions come their way. Keeping students on their toes through random questioning will amaze you. The trick hinges on praise rather than judgment.

One quick caveat. Getting to know your students is paramount. We want to avoid adding stress to their lives. I always start with concepts that students will be comfortable with, so even those reserved teens feel more comfortable getting involved. Start slow, and you'll be impressed with the confidence it builds.

Once a week at least. When I began my career, I didn't truly under-stand assessments. I even complained at lunch that my third-grade class seemed to forget things almost as fast as I had taught them. One of my colleagues said, "Craig, they're in third grade, not college calculus." He was correct. Teaching anything one time is like learning to drive a manual transmission (see below). Learning must be done in a step by step fashion for growth to occur. Also, authenticity/real-time practice is critical. When I started teaching my son Cole to drive my Honda Accord 6-speed, I was reminded of this. Even though he'd done some driving before, he still hadn't mastered all that a "stick" entails (like being on a real road). One day, he got pulled over by the police for not putting his turn signal on, and I, as the not-very-receptive parent/teacher, was rather gruff about his error. Cole said, "Dad, are you kidding? Using the turn signal was the last thing on my mind; I was worried about stalling!" In retrospect, I should have remembered that I had a similar first experience by almost crashing into a pole and running into the car dealership. My point is to make sure you repeat information often in a way that is: positive, rewarding, praiseworthy, and fun. Even if students have been assessed already, revisiting concepts often is simply effective teaching while also promoting the importance of mastery.

A student or two a day. As students enter the class, I randomly pick one or two and have them tell me something important they learned in one of our previous classes. The first time I tried this with two students, both stared at me with a deer-in-the-headlights stare and mumbled incoherently. After the three of us laughed, I explained my purpose and repeated the message to the class. This technique, where nobody knows who will be selected the next day, prepares students to think and speak before entering the room.

Please make it fun. When students are young, they are constantly learning through play. We would never think of having five and six-year-old children just sitting and listening for long periods. We get them excited, moving, interacting, and learning, even when they don't think that's happening. We shouldn't change because of the age of a student. Students feel motivated to succeed when lessons are unique, inspiring, and different. They see things as a journey to explore instead of as a chore.

Training the brain is a process. When I started coaching cross country, I knew little about the sport. Even though I'd been an avid runner for a long time, coaching high school students was a different story. I picked up a book called, *The Running Formula* by Jack Daniels (not the whiskey). Over the next thirteen years, I probably read and re-read sections of the book thirty to forty times. That repetition helped me understand and apply the information to my athletes. A combination of the examples above or what you learn from others can help in the process. With some experimentation, you'll create your own "train your brain" methods to enhance learning.

You can do it:

1. Other than tests and quizzes, what instructional techniques do you use to ensure students retain content and lessons previously taught?
2. How frequently do you return to material that has already been assessed?

Get going:

1. During a lesson, try one of the activities outlined in this chapter.
2. Afterward, have students reflect on the activity.

• CHAPTER 19 •
UBD

There are many things we don't understand and many ways to unlock the brain and maximize function. Don't ever let anybody tell you it can't be done."

— Sally Fryer Dietz

I 'm guessing many educators who saw this title, "UBD," thought of the teaching framework, *Understanding by Design* by Jay McTighe. Many school districts, mine included, have implemented the UBD template to form curriculum and lesson design. It can be a very effective way to plan content and lessons. Plus, there are countless resources online. Rather than rave about the process, I encourage you to explore how it works and speak to your leadership team about its benefits. Now on to **U**nderstanding **B**rain **D**evelopment.

Reflecting on my youth, I could have benefited as a learner from the UBD (my acronym) methodology. Unfortunately, I struggled academically. My Uncle Bernie, rest his soul, always told me so in rather blunt terms. He didn't parse words. When I was a teenager, he mentioned how I was a spoiled brat. My favorite line of his (stated "diplomatically") is, "Craig needs to get his... together." Frankly, he was right.

Uncle Bernie's willingness to be blunt might strike some of you as unkind, but his purpose of motivating me always resonated with me. I didn't want to do poorly in high school. My maturity level and brain development just weren't ready for an extended period of sitting, listening to lectures, and teacher-centered instruction. Luckily, as college progressed, my brain was prepared to learn material I deemed necessary.

Let my experience remind you that each child we teach is different. We've all heard that before, but putting that thinking into action can be challenging. It's easy to see some students sitting attentively for long stretches and thinking they are doing great. While that may be the case, today, too many variables impact someone's schooling to make such a blanket statement. Knowing that each of our student's brains is wired differently for learning should be paramount. The following strategies aren't earth-shattering but quick tips that can help build successful teaching habits.

Stay on point. The brains of children and teens can only process so much information at one time. Especially the case if you're striving for mastery. Earlier in my career, I was guilty of teaching too much, too fast. The challenges of getting through every unit, all the content, and assessing all the time, seemed most important. In reality, that was flawed thinking. It's true that while some students may have some success, that's not the goal. We want all students to prosper. When covering content, ensure students understand precisely what you expect from them and why it's essential before moving on. Ask them questions and have a dialogue about what you've taught. Once you feel that each student understands clearly, you can move on to new material.

Teach new material in segments. I recall the first time a golf club was put in my hand. It was like *Happy Gilmore,* and *Caddyshack* revisited. Balls flew all over the place, yelling "fore" over and over in the hopes that I didn't hit somebody. My lack of previous skill acquisition made learning golf much more complicated than if I had practiced the steps of a proper golf swing. Sequential learning, movement in stages, zooming in to challenging areas and checking for understanding exist in every content area. Just as I needed to keep my eye on the golf ball, most students need cues to understand how to process and apply learning in a relevant manner. You'll have to break things into parts in those areas where knowledge is progressive and continuous.

Allow and encourage students to connect about the lesson during breaks or testing for understanding. We are wired for communication. We know how easy it is for teachers and administrators to focus on the "that class is excellent; look how quiet they are." It seems clear that having an attentive classroom (that doesn't mean quiet) has its place, and I'm not suggesting constant chatter is good. But hearing just one voice in one tone can severely limit how much learning occurs. Also, students interacting with each other allows for valuable feedback that one person may be unable to provide. Finally, the shared moments among students will improve the climate and build community in your class.

Give them tons of wins, scattered with a few tough losses. Vary the difficulty of your lessons. Starting with the material they have a background in can ease kids into a task and lead to the psychological advantage that success can bring. Teaching through incremental adjustments can be a great confidence builder. On the other hand, adding too much information too quickly, which is too complex or uninteresting, will lead to students giving up and maybe even losing hope in learning altogether. It's that Art of Teaching coming up again. One other key point; please mix in some very challenging work. Making the content too easy may seem like a great idea. Students feel good, and their grades follow that trend. Unfortunately, it never prepares them for more challenging material. Having students only seeing success with their lessons will leave them ill-prepared for more challenging work. It will also impact their confidence in taking risks when work is hard, and they struggle since they've never become acclimated to it.

Measure students in different ways; allow for reflection about the best assessment options for each student. I'm not advocating twenty-five tests, quizzes, or lessons for twenty-five students. Using technology, group work, writing, discussions, tests, projects, etc., are all great ways to see what students might need or what they've mastered. Even if a quiz, test, or project is the final assessment tool, you should still use multiple ways to measure growth. One quick caveat: please avoid using every tech tool or assessment variation. While it may seem creative, it will cause "confusion overload" when students have no idea what's coming next.

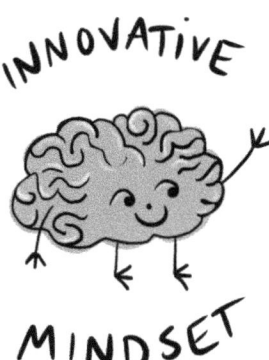

Share your vision of why a lesson is essential. Do students know what you'd like them to achieve or why you believe it matters? I'm not speaking just about an objective on the board. Too often, we think a posted standard is the same as articulating a goal. Objectives and standards matter, but without explicit, purposeful instruction, they are just words on a board or piece of paper. We must clearly explain *why* a lesson, assignment, or quick break matters.

Keep brain development in mind as you plan your lessons. Adults generally have a lifetime of experience and a mature brain that can organize thoughts, prioritize tasks, and understand how learning occurs. Children and teenagers rarely have those acquired skills. If we try to understand how their brains work, we can shape content delivery in an exciting and meaningful way.

You can do it:

1. When you reflect on your best lessons, what steps did you take to ensure students understood the content?
2. How do you segment or develop your units to excite your class?

Get going:

1. On a challenging assignment, give students alternative methods to show mastery.
2. After completion, do a quick think/pair/share to find out what challenged them.

• CHAPTER 20 •
DO THEY KNOW IT?

Dedicated to my friend,
Michael Sandler

> *Learning should rarely be defined as a one-and-done attempt at what students may know. It should be a journey of continuous exploration and wonder."*

Thanksgiving of 2020 was coming to a close. One of my dear friends, Michael Sandler, stopped over to visit. Because of COVID-19, we were out on the deck having our usual chats about education. We frequently talked about education whenever we'd get together. Because of our constant banter, this chapter is dedicated to him. I'm not sure how the conversation got on what our students remember from our teaching, but once we started going off, he said, "Craig, you've got to put this in your book."

We don't need tons of data to recall everything we don't remember from our formative years. I can attest that my recollection is close to zero. I recall many sports, dating, friends, trouble I'd get in, and other silly teenage behavior acts. As for actual learning, it's my Spanish numbers, *Catcher in the Rye*, and bench pressing on a universal machine in P.E. class.

There are scientific and non-scientific reasons why this occurs. As fantastic as our brains are, they aren't wired to remember every bit of information; instead, they focus on what we deem most important. Our teaching system has been on the non-scientific side of the equation: do well on the test, get good grades, forget what we learned, repeat. In education, we have heard, "We have all this content to teach; there isn't enough time in the day to master every concept." While that may seem like a legitimate answer, take a pause and consider if you'd like to learn something that doesn't have value.

As an example from the previous paragraph, our class was reflecting on the results of our quiz. One of the students mentioned, "Shap, I wish you would have told us the quiz was coming. I didn't have time to study." I replied, "Why should I tell you when the quiz is? You should already know the information. Once the quiz was up, would you truthfully look over the content again?" She replied, "No!" My point is simple. We have to focus on delivering the best and most meaningful version of content possible. So here we go.

Figure out what's important. When I reflect on the thousands of lessons I've taught, it's easy to believe they all carried the same value and intrigue. That's just not the case. Some content is more important than others. What we teach and how meaningful it is will depend on many variables: previous knowledge, vocabulary, the complexity of concepts, required curriculum, and, honestly, our love of the material. Students will quickly see if what we are teaching matters to us. I'm not suggesting every moment be special. Consider when planning: what will carry the best bang for the buck. An excellent method is simply thinking: is what I'm teaching exciting if I were the student? With that in mind, here are four quick questions that can assist in planning:

1. Does this content or lesson matter to my students and me?
2. Will students truly value this content?
3. Is there a connection to their life, or might there be down the road?
4. Will the majority of students enjoy or embrace the material?

Plan conservatively. I'll be the first to admit that I've frequently planned too many things and then gotten frustrated when only half of my plan got taught. Instead, to plan accordingly, reflect on the following: "What must students know, what would you like them to know, and what would be a great bonus for them to know?" Of course, each teacher can use techniques that suit their style. But please don't feel overwhelmed with the idea, "I have to teach everything now."

Keep them guessing and remembering. A large portion of my teaching day is focused on wellness. As somebody passionate about the field, I'm proud that so many young people are seeing how beneficial it can be. Unfortunately, with so much misinformation available at their fingertips, I need to keep them on their toes. I'll randomly ask students to explain and demonstrate some key concepts we learned in the first week of class. Yes, I catch a few students with their eyes looking down. Yet with a bit of practice, it leads to a confident student who has mastery of the material. I've even had students say, "Shap, we covered that already. Why are you asking that of me now?" I always respond, "Do you know the answer?" Most of the time, they answer it correctly and smile.

I realize that every educator has different methods for assessing their students. Many excellent techniques will work. Even if it's impossible to have all students use everything we teach, our ability to be creative in our lessons goes a long way to successful teaching.

You can do it:

1. How do you ensure students truly understand and remember those crucial concepts?
2. What strategies have you shared with others that enable them to try new ideas?

Get going:

1. Do a random Q and A session about past material taught.
2. After completion, use a board write, gallery walk, or other interactive activity to assess the results.

° CHAPTER 21 °
CHANCES = SUCCESS

> " *I have so many students who would just give up on school if they saw there was no way to turn the power back on their grades.*"
>
> — Sam Rangel

One of my first teaching positions was a six-week, long-term substitute job. During our classes, especially those earliest in the day, it wasn't uncommon for students to wander in unprepared, turn in work late, or show minimal motivation in class.

As a new teacher, I'd ask questions about how to deal with these situations. While I can't remember every word, I've always thought about the valuable tips those fantastic teachers mentioned. To paraphrase some of their comments: "Craig, you'll get many suggestions from experts in the field. Some will be useful; others not so much. We use the questions below as a guide. They will come up frequently no matter where or what you teach."

Chances = Success

1. What are you trying to assess?
2. How will you build relationships so that kids want to thrive in your class or school?
3. Is late work better than no work?
4. What circumstances are involved in a student's life?
5. Are students improving each day, each week, and each year?

The five questions listed above have wandered through my brain over and over. I'm grateful that somebody was wise enough to share them early in my career. Before covering those critical points, I'd like to briefly mention "Fearless," one of the last chapters. It relates so much to the issues above. It's an example of breaking through with a student. The chapter would never have been written had we not given our relationship a second chance. Now to those five questions.

What are you trying to assess? It may seem strange to mention this since so much teaching revolves around best practices to evaluate students. We know that objectives and standards can provide a framework for success. Still, the best-aligned standards won't work if varied, positive instruction is missing. To truly measure achievement, multiple opportunities must occur.

As adults, we know how easy it is to forget things if they are only taught once. Think about those same concepts for students. Frequently, students have multiple content areas to study, homework to complete, and other stressors besides school. If students are only assessed one time, it seems clear that long-term acquisition will be lacking.

How will you build relationships so students thrive in your class or school? Much of the first section covered relationship building and getting off to a good start. I value it so much that here are some more ideas to consider.

1. Start with content that ALL students can succeed with.
2. Praise and give meaningful feedback.
3. Learn names quickly and use them often.
4. Get students comfortable talking about themselves.
5. Create lessons that promote conversations, collaboration, and taking risks.
6. Promote dialogue, questions, and culture building that go beyond the content you teach.
7. Provide opportunities for sharing their culture.

Are students improving each day? Each week? Each year? We know that students have incredible variations in where they start, so our ability to focus on consistent and measurable growth is critical. Also, development should be evaluated in more than just one metric. Social, physical, academic, and emotional forward growth tells a much bigger picture than just one lateness, poor quiz, or even one great project. Even though the buzz term "growth mindset" has taken hold, it has an essential value in the context of progressive student learning. Here are some fundamental guidelines to consider:

- Look at the work you're assigning. Projects take more time than simple Q and A.
- Ask students what they think might be a reasonable time frame for the completion of projects.
- Use your results as a guide to keep going or make a change. Data should be a huge part of driving instruction.
- Always focus on communicating your expectations. Don't assume students know what your expectations are.

- Put policies/guidelines in place that are written, spoken, and discussed in class.

After reading this chapter, we should meet students' challenges with empathy, kindness, and compassion. Let's always provide opportunities for growth, improved learning, and better relationships.

You can do it:

1. How do you currently provide multiple chances for students to succeed? Is your policy flexible or written in stone?
2. In what ways do your students feel empowered in their learning?

Get going:

1. When assigning work, ask students what deadlines and parameters best fit their needs. Work together to come to a fair and equitable solution.
2. With younger students, give them options around how they show their work, socialize with their peers, and reflect on their work.

• CHAPTER 22 •
Move It

At 10:40 every day, our department eats brunch. Yes, brunch! I'd always bring the same items: a can of chicken breast, yogurt, an apple, and water. Even with those bland foods, I'd be close to nodding off after about ten to fifteen minutes while sitting down. My coworkers would laugh that I could close my eyes so quickly after sitting and eating. After this short brunch break, the bell would ring, and our students would enter our locker room to prepare for physical education. One of my students would frequently come into our office, sit down, and say, "I don't know, Shap, I'm so tired. I just had a huge lunch. Not sure I'm feeling it today." I'd usually respond with snarky comments about working hard, being motivated, and eating healthy.

Fast forward to the Winter and Spring of 2018. Since I had Health right after lunch, I remembered my daily siestas and how easy it was to veg out when sitting down. That recollection and the student's banter about being tired and not being up for doing work made me think that many other students probably felt the same way.

I recalled a trick I'd read online as I entered my third-period Health class. The teacher had a bell set up in their class. If students seemed bored, uninterested, or tired, she'd go up to the bell and ring it. Students would immediately get up from their desks and stretch, do a movement activity or mingle for a minute with their peers. That little trick created tremendous energy, and the consistent change of pace never allowed them to get bored. I don't know why I didn't think of something like that sooner, but it's been a hugely positive development in my class. While I don't use a bell, there are hundreds of ways to get students actively moving.

There is science behind the value of movement and its incredible value to the body and brain. In years past, educators focused on younger students needing breaks from class, but now the research shows the value for all grades, especially if the gaps are short and meaningful. I mentioned earlier that fifteen to twenty minutes of instruction is a good starting point. Follow this with a few minutes of movement or socialization. This will, of course, depend on the length of your class and grade level. The longer the class, the more frequent the movement needs to be. Yet, for many students, getting them active needs to be explained.

I mention this solely because most kids would jump out of their seats to do something fun and movement-oriented in the elementary and beginning middle grades. As students reach later middle and high school grades, there is a tendency to sit down, listen, be compliant, and often be satisfied at best or disinterested at worst. Initially, when I mentioned we would move, it was, "Shap, do we have to?" But by making this a daily habit, smiles have become the norm. Knowing that even a short break is coming helps students stay focused. After speaking with many teens, they say that getting that quick break allows them to stay motivated, while looking forward to getting out of their seats. For those who think that getting them back on task would be difficult, it's quite the opposite. Think about many of your professional development sessions that go on and on with no break. Even though we might be quiet, it's only out of respect, not because we enjoy sitting for long periods. The same thing exists for students. If you make it a habit, it becomes no different from other daily procedures, such as exit tickets, pre-class assignments, and music in class.

The hardest thing about keeping kids moving is keeping kids moving. There will be times when they are engaged in learning, and you won't want them to stop. In those instances, stay the course. Movement and taking breaks are not meant to be so structured that it ruins the flow and excitement of your teaching. Nobody would expect you to have students stop in the middle of a test to walk around the room.

Instead of being stuck to a schedule, try being vigilant with student body language and your sense of the classroom. If you're looking at a bunch of blank stares or sense that students need a break, have them get up even for a minute or two. There are endless activities that specifically promote movement. At the end of this chapter, I've provided a QR code of games that I've used. I plan on adding more as I try new things. Here are a few helpful hints to consider when it comes to movement.

To plan or not to plan - This is an individual decision based on your teaching style. If you're the kind of teacher that sticks strictly to your plan, setting up movement in class becomes easy. The only downside is that you'll lose the spontaneity of when students may need to move when you didn't plan for it. If you're not a planner, you'll have more flexibility, but avoid using movement to extreme levels.

Think about the goal - Sometimes, my goal is to give them a quick de-stress, socialization break. Other times, it's much more intentional about a learning objective. In an earlier chapter, I discussed the concept of being purposeful. That is important when you think about movement. You'll develop this skill the more you try it in class. Practice makes perfect.

Give students a voice - As you'll read throughout the book, giving students a voice is non-negotiable. The same holds for getting them moving. While I suggest you initially come up with ideas, after a while, it's empowering to allow students to pick. I've asked students, "What's our movement for today?" In an effort to be funny, some will say, "Shap, let's just go for a 60-minute walk today!" Even though I'll often nix that idea, it shows that they want to move and feel comfortable joking around.

Games, Games - Because of my natural background in Health and Physical Education, games have long been a part of my classroom instruction. Children and teens love the cooperation and competition that come from playing games. While some might think of games in a non-academic manner, that doesn't have to be the case. Depending on your objectives, games can reinforce mastery, build cooperation for learning new material, and promote movement in class, which is the focus of this chapter. For those who want to try new ideas, I've included a QR Code to access descriptions of some of the games I've used in class. I'll be adding more, so I hope you check out those.

Promoting movement in class is naturally fun for everyone. Your class will rarely get bored, and you'll reap positive rewards if you do activities that revolve around learning. Don't worry if things don't go perfectly. Just as in many aspects of teaching and learning, the process and growth matter most.

You can do it:

1. What activities do you currently use in class to promote student movement? How frequently do you use them?
2. Have you asked students what ideas they have for movement? If so, what have they suggested?

Get going:

1. Pick an activity where students are actively moving around the room. It can be one of the activities described in this chapter or something you have learned from another teacher.
2. After implementing the activity, ask students how it went and how it might be improved.

CHAPTER 23
10,000 Steps

Movement around the class promotes higher effort levels,
more interaction with students, and it's even good exercise.

E ven though fitness has been a passion of mine since childhood, I never thought about how many steps I took in a day until my wife surprised me on my 50th birthday with a Fitbit Surge. Having heard others talk about 10,000, 15,000, and 20,000 steps, I figured I'd be easily near the top with my job being a wellness educator! When I saw 4,252 on my first day, it was shocking. On the following day, with different classes, I calculated why the number was so low. While I rarely sat at the computer, the watch confirmed that I was mainly moving around in a five- to ten-foot space in the front of the class. This discovery signaled a time for a change.

When I earned my Master's Degree in Educational Leadership, a common theme focused on teacher effectiveness. One quality of outstanding teachers is their frequent movement during class. They could change the computer screen or pull up a document for students to view, but most of their time was spent engaging students. Even though too much movement can be distracting, intentional action/movement will help students understand the material and build those vital connections.

One of my best recollections of teacher movement's power on an audience was from a hands-on experience in professional development. Our staff attended a meeting on a topic I still can't remember because of the lack of mixed instruction. Finally, after ending, we were given a few minutes to stretch. After we recovered from the boredom, another presenter took center stage. In stark contrast to the initial experience, she moved around the room while discussing the topic. She demonstrated a great sense of when to interject and proceed. In addition to her movement, there were stark differences in body language and behaviors compared to our initial presenter. Through her presence, those previously on their phone turned them off and focused on the task.

I can't stress how relevant that last sentence is to consider. Education is changing. Technology is everywhere, and it's here to stay. Moving around your room and having proximity to students is mandatory for excellent instruction. Higher engagement and reduced off-task behaviors are reinforced when a teacher stops to chat with students or even gives them a quick stare from across the room.

For example, I recall being in Mr. Black's room during my junior year in high school. He would lock eyes with me, sometimes smile, but also provide a "death stare" that was code for "Craig, get back to work." If he were just sitting behind his desk, I would never have refocused on the task.

The benefit of connecting with challenging, hard-to-reach students is even more significant than reducing off-task behavior. If you're only at your desk or standing in front of the room, those "hide-under-the-radar" kids will be prone to a lack of involvement. I can think of many instances where I've gotten to know quiet and reserved students by moving around and interacting with them. Yes, some were probably caught off guard or even initially intimidated. But after they realized I cared about them, those concerns disappeared.

Early on, we covered the concept of being purposeful. Movement, both from a teacher and student, falls under that category. By no means do you always need to be moving and circulating the room. Plan accordingly with your objectives for that day. Occasionally, it's perfectly okay to watch interaction from your desk. Sometimes I'll watch kids present in front of the class, and it's awe-inspiring. That said, if you increase your movement time even a little bit, your whole class will benefit, and you'll see some positive results, both academically and socially. Just as a finishing thought, remember to have achievable goals if you count steps during your classroom day. Use your first initial days as a benchmark. Giving a test will lower your step count, while other specific activities will naturally increase them. Use a combination of days to get the best estimate. Once you have some numbers written down, go for short improvements every week. Before you know it, 10,000 or more will be the norm.

You can do it:

1. How much time in your teaching day do you estimate you're moving around the room?
2. Have you thought about why it's essential to be actively moving during a lesson? What shapes your thinking on this?

Get going:

1. The next time students work independently or in small groups, make it a point to ask as many students as possible if they need help, how the lesson is going, or even what's something special that's coming up in their lives.
2. Write down some of the information you learned, discuss your findings with the class, or take notes for later lesson planning.

• CHAPTER 24 •

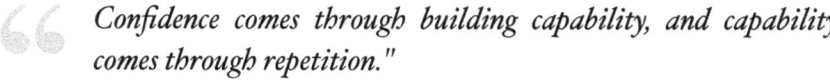

Find Your GO-To

> *Confidence comes through building capability, and capability comes through repetition."*
>
> — Angela Watson

I love post-it notes! The different colors, sizes, and shapes make them a great learning tool for any age group. More importantly, it's the ease at which you can make them a daily, fun way for any student to show creativity while still learning. For example, when students enter my classroom, they find a table with post-it notes and pick up a color of their choice. On a post-it note, they write a response to a question or comment found on our Easel of Excellence board. We do a quick discussion or other activity to get them actively thinking. Sometimes we've even used them for an exit ticket or as a pay-it-forward closure. When I started the initial entering of class ideas about six years ago, I never thought it would be one of my main "go-to" ways because of how simplistic it seemed. But it is precisely that simplicity that makes it quickly repeatable daily.

Having at least one "go-to" idea that you do daily will provide structure for your students, create an atmosphere of high expectations, and foster a positive space. It may seem easy to dismiss a simple post-it note, but many educators have a routine or "go-to" way of preparing for the day or ending a class. Whether you have one or more "go-to" ways to connect with students, this chapter is about finding and enhancing those routines.

A typical day in many classrooms is hectic. Between emails, phone calls, assessments, activities, and the pace of the day, it becomes easy to lose track of everything going on. When I started using the Easel of Excellence board and Post-it notes, the structure helped me and the class get centered. In other words, that simple, quick task carried over to our main lesson by starting something fun, positive, and non-stressful. Thinking back to our successes as students, it's not hard to guess that we had much more enjoyment during our formative years when our teachers eased us into learning, had a consistent theme, and ensured we felt confident.

How will your daily "go-to" ideas positively impact students? Finding the answer to this is a critical question. Our teaching should promote growth, socialization, wellness, and academic excellence. In some instances, you'll be fortunate to find something that hits kids in all these ways. But even only one domain is a big step in the right direction.

Whenever you have a daily activity, there are always questions you need to consider. These questions aren't all-inclusive but are a starting point to help you plan accordingly. No 100 percent correct answer exists, so don't stress if you have to rethink your solutions. They will change as your teaching adapts.

- Are you using a "go-to" as an introduction or exit-ticket type of activity?
- Is there a specific objective that needs to be accomplished?
- Do your students know the purpose of what you're doing?
- Are you planning on having the activity assessed? If yes, will it be graded: always, on certain occasions, or never?
- Can the "go-to" be measurable with data? If so, what outcomes are you looking for?

Any time you start something new, there will be a learning curve. Even in my example of post-it notes, things look different now than on day one. Please don't throw something out if it doesn't work perfectly. Just like we'd tell students to keep at it, our philosophy should follow that same mantra. Even if it falls flat, laugh it off, and realize your initial idea might need some tweaking. Also, you want to avoid the "hamster wheel" of constantly trying new things. While taking those risks is part of effective teaching, we don't want so many new ideas that time gets wasted. In addition, the class won't develop a sense of purpose behind what you're trying to do. A much better approach is getting some feedback from students, as well as your analysis.

I wanted to throw out five speedy "go-to" ideas that may get you off to a successful start. Again, these are of the simple variety and don't take tons of planning. Even though I mentioned having them as a daily routine, they can be mixed and matched together. No matter how you adapt them to your class, they are great ways to experiment.

1. A quick personal question on the board, easel, or whatever format you use. You can start with questions as simple as your favorite season and progress to something like, "Tell me a positive quality that you have." Even a positive word of the day can be a great starter.

2. I got this fabulous idea from my good friend Kati Dreben. She is an incredible teacher and massage therapist. We were chatting about an activity I was doing in the class called "one thing." The concept was based on some of the previous conversations we had about having our best life. I had given the class six questions to ponder about their lives. They were: One thing you're proud of. One thing that brings you joy. One thing that causes you stress. One thing you would do to make the world a better place. One thing you'd love to improve on. One thing you'd change about school. It's a great way to get students of all ages to think about themselves. She mentioned that it might be cool to have students grab an expo marker or other writing object and write a quick thought on the board about what they like, something that makes them unique, their favorite hobby, or other ideas that come to mind. Not only are students up and moving, but the sharing component is also precious. Plus, the time spent discussing their responses can be driven by both you and your students.

3. Guess the song. As a huge music fan, students always ask me to play music no matter what we do. The beginning of class, end of class, or during a break are good times to play music. You can try different genres and ask students to guess the name of a song, which is an excellent ice-breaker.

4. Use a daily, quick stretch, exercise, or something to get students out of their chairs. Those simple movements break up a routine, get students' brains/bodies going, are fun, and become a welcome change from sitting.

5. Think, pair, share. Yes, I know this has been around for years. It's still a fantastic way to have students connect. One caveat I

use is avoiding having them talk to the same person repeatedly. While it can be a little daunting initially, allowing students to get comfortable with just their friends can be a hard habit to break.

As I was writing this chapter, I realized how often I'd done the same daily activities with students. I can't say it's the end-all, be-all of classroom engagement, but it creates a specific pattern of comfort that helps students feel at home in class.

You can do it:

1. Do you have a "go-to" idea/activity that is part of your daily teaching? What is it?
2. Have your students had a role in some of your rituals? If so, which ones?

Get going:

1. Get feedback from your students on what type of daily, quick activity would enhance their experience in class.
2. Try one of their suggestions and see how it works.

CHAPTER 25

Too Much, Too Little, Just Right

 Slowing down for ourselves and for our students."

— Alex Shevin Venet & Arlene Elizabeth Casimir

"Hey, Shap! Can we go for a walk today? Can you help us film a video? Can we push the quiz back to the next class?" Each year, there are a hundred things on my plate. Whether it is tons of new technology, filming videos, or any other endeavors, it can be so draining when being super busy is the norm. I'm guessing that for many of you, my words ring true.

Even with our motives being all about helping students, please realize that something will suffer anytime we spread ourselves too thin. Maybe not immediately, but over time it's impossible to sustain our best when we try to do everything for everyone.

I was recently speaking with one of our school's newest hires. She mentioned the challenges of juggling so many teaching responsibilities and asked for tips for navigating all we have to do. I said, "I'm so glad you brought up this subject. Part of my New Year's Resolution is to focus on what's most important. I'm going to streamline my lesson." Hopefully, this chapter can highlight some ways to make that happen. As a side note, I hope my friend and the fantastic teacher Nancy K.B. Berkovitz will read and re-read this chapter. She will understand where I'm coming from.

Plan Simple - In my early years, I was guilty of "everything must be done today." I'd over-plan my lessons instead of keeping things simple for students. Educators often feel every tidbit of a lesson plan must be completed for success. That's rarely the case. I now highlight or bold the "must-do" concepts before moving on.

What's difficult and what's easy - Think about our experiences learning new material. When technology became a part of education, many people struggled (and still do) to master the hundreds of new applications. That's no different for students. Always reflect on what might be easy, moderate, or complicated for students to grasp. By doing this, you'll avoid stress for your students and yourself. As you're planning lessons, consider possible hurdles, successes, time, and assessment strategies. No rule states that every concept must have the same time allowance, grade, or difficulty level.

Talk to your class - Allowing and promoting feedback shapes engagement. As I've mentioned frequently throughout the book, many students seek compliance if you allow that to happen. They have learned through time that it's easier to listen than to get deep into a conversation. I'm in the middle of our fitness unit as of this writing. During our last class, I must have had 20+ questions on exercises, losing weight, and finding something students like. This happened because of the constant, and I mean constant, prodding for them to seek help. Your dialogue with students will allow you to plan accordingly for future lessons. Maybe your outstanding teaching has led to quicker mastery than you initially thought, or you might have to scale back a bit and push off a topic for a day or two. Students are the best guide on when to move forward. Allowing students to have a voice and promoting lots of conversation will improve their ability to feel comfortable. Once one student jumps on board, others will follow. With that said, I strongly encourage giving lots of praise, smiles, and feedback.

Relax - The Covid pandemic caused thousands of educators to feel stressed about the material they had to cover. In my district, we had to change schedules multiple times, which forced us to adjust accordingly. While I can't speak for other educators, I've learned to relax if something wasn't done at the exact moment as planned. If you're rushed, anxious, and upset that you're not getting far enough in a lesson, students will pick up on this and may feel unnecessary stress. Education isn't a linear journey, as Covid has taught us. It's much more about controlling what we can and adapting when necessary.

You may feel uncomfortable scaling back to a more manageable schedule. It's hard to make changes that seem like less is more. I encourage you to start small and give it a try. Students will have less stress and appreciate your patience and willingness to get the temperature right.

You can do it:

1. How do you plan your lessons, so all students have a clear understanding of the content?
2. What benefits do you see from streamlining your lesson plans?

Get going:

1. Pick a lesson or two that may be challenging to students. Speak to them about how much time and assistance they need. Then, based on initial results, adjust as necessary.
2. Discuss with your class how to best adjust the difficulty level of work. Then put the plan into action.

CHAPTER 26
EMPOWER YOURSELF
EMPOWER YOUR STUDENTS

"Giving students the power to learn will create a classroom of excited teachers and students."

In section one, you'll recall that one of the "E" words of the "3Es" was empowering. While I discussed the value of empowerment, I've dedicated this chapter to the process because empowerment, just by its nature, promotes collaboration, confidence, risk-taking, and academic performance.

Sharing control of the classroom with students isn't easy. Teacher-led instruction has been part of the educational climate for a long time. Some of this is by habit or just that it has been accepted. While I've never thought this instructional method should be our singular teaching methodology, it seemed okay before many tools were at our disposal. Today, it's different. Allowing students to have a role in the decision-making will take your teaching to new heights. As a young teacher, I couldn't imagine giving so many choices and decisions on assessment. From my experience, those positive choices have impacted academic growth, and the value of learning across all domains of learning for students is evident. To get you thinking about your classroom, I like using the "five do" questions as a guide.

1. **Do students always know why you want them to be empowered in their learning?** Explaining why you're asking them to be risk-takers and giving them opportunities to have a choice will shape their willingness to take on challenges without fear of failure.

2. **Do you provide opportunities in your daily lessons for more personal, creative ways to learn?** As a huge advocate of student choice, I've seen firsthand the value of giving students time to experiment. No matter what subject we teach, students need time to explore areas that might interest them. I recall having students begin a project of their choice using the fantastic application, Canva. Their work and creativity led to new explorations and learning that might never have happened if I'd just stayed the course. Opening up many paths to success reduces the chance of getting stuck on one rocky road.

3. **Do you explain how empowering them relates to your curriculum?** Empowering students isn't about saying, "I'm going to empower you to do whatever you like." Instead, it's about bridging your mandated standards and objectives with those lessons that improve academic performance, cooperation, and higher-level thinking. This kind of teaching creates a setting where high expectations become the norm for students.

4. **Do you provide frequent reflective questions?** Empowered teaching is a style that helps students to be aware of their learning. Lessons or units should contain "why," "what," and "how" questions for students to answer, thereby consolidating the main ideas from the student's point of view.

5. **Do you start slowly?** As I mentioned earlier, my experiences with empowering students had been fraught with mistakes, do-overs, grading mishaps, and other issues that wouldn't have happened if I had slowed down. The choice for students must be a gradual progression. Even with the possibility that advanced students may get things quickly, don't fret. Give them time to help those who are struggling. These strategies become a great socialization and leadership tool. If that's not something you feel comfortable with, I've often promoted further research into the topic we are covering. No grades are given, so it becomes their learning opportunity for mastery.

Promoting a class around choice is about showing flexibility with deadlines, being patient, providing guidance, and stressing the quality of work over just turning it in. It's essential to understand that sometimes getting excellent work will take more time than is usually given. With that said, each teacher's guidelines for due dates are often an individual choice. If you recall, section one focused on strong relationships. As you engage students with challenging work, it will help immensely to consider who might need more time and who can advance more quickly.

Keep in mind that how you start this journey will differ from your colleagues. That's okay since it will be the same for students. Actual change won't be achieved in a day or a week. It is a consistent willingness to keep pushing, even when it is much easier to stay the course.

You can do it:

1. How much of your current lessons consist of empowering your students?
2. What lessons could be adapted to foster student empowerment?

Get going:

1. Find a colleague who has tried this kind of instruction and discuss ways to work together on a lesson or project.
2. Pick one upcoming lesson or even part of one. Then adjust it so students see the potential learning outcomes of being empowered.

• CHAPTER 27 •

Dear Students,

A word after a word after a word is power."

— Margaret Atwood

T he irony that writing has become such a big part of my classroom instruction makes me smile. In high school, I avoided writing like the plague. A triple excuse of asking to go to the bathroom, not having a pencil, or forgetting my notebook was my typical (yet not consistently successful) way of not putting words on paper.

Luckily, that's changed for the better. Part of my initial enjoyment of writing came from the many letters I'd write for those athletes I was coaching. I learned about the importance of writing while coaching with my friend Andy. He would jot down reflective words on index cards to our wrestlers. When I initially read the notes, I thought, *"Why not just tell them what you're writing?"* But, as many of our athletes read his thoughtful words, the personal involvement of writing carried a huge positive weight. Those deliberately placed words reminded our athletes how much we were vested in their success.

When I became the Girls' Cross Country coach, I followed Andy's lead by using the examples he demonstrated while we coached together. Notes became part of our culture, celebration, and reflection. Just a few sentences brought smiles to our athletes and their parents. Also, the learning that occurred when we reviewed their performances was just as critical. This same idea can be even more impactful in your classroom.

Believe it or not, coaching a team is not all that different from teaching a class. Just as you want your team to bond, share and thrive, the same holds for any classroom. For example, during the 2017 school year, I wanted to say goodbye to a fantastic group of teens. I thought, "Why not write it down?" My goal was to create a class letter and encourage them to continue their unique learning journey. The trick was to keep the messages pertinent for all students and confined to one page or less. Reviewing the document, it struck me that we had covered many of the suggestions during the year. They loved it! Below is the actual letter. You can adjust it as it fits your needs and your students.

————

Reflection Letter 2017

Dear Students,

Thank you! I appreciate your positive and constructive feedback. Your work and unique interactions have made the time together memorable and rewarding.

Below are some key points moving forward. They can guide you as you progress throughout high school and beyond. My door is always open, and I hope you'll visit frequently.

The Six to Consider

1. **Be happy and open-minded** - We are different in so many ways that a one-size-fits-all recipe doesn't work. We are all unique, and that's a great thing. With that said, having an open mind and showing positivity is a happiness creator.
2. **Chart your course** - Listening to others is important. Many teachers, as well as your parents, play an essential role in your future. In the end, you must find your path to success. That

road will have some hurdles along the way. Remember, mistakes can be helpful if we learn from them and adjust.

3. **Pay it Forward** - Improving the lives of others leads to a more fruitful and enjoyable life. When you Pay it Forward, it comes back to you in a meaningful way. Little things, like holding a door, helping somebody with their homework, or even taking out the trash, can be easy to do and offer huge dividends. Keep it simple and pass it along.

4. **Get off the phone** - Phones have become part of our lives. For better or worse, that won't be changing anytime soon; with that said, face-to-face interactions matter. Nothing can take the place of seeing a smile or just a simple acknowledgment. You'll be amazed how communicating with others in person leads to stronger relationships. Also, interactions make a strong impression when interviewing or speaking with groups.

5. **Don't sweat the small stuff** - Most of what we get carried away with usually means little over the long run. Count to ten and think about the energy and time you're consuming on something minor. We've shared many examples in class, and I hope they connected with you. Focus on the big picture.

6. **Lastly, do your best** - Not because you want a reward or a grade, but because you seek to improve and grow. Twenty years from now, it won't matter that you had an "A" in our class. Yes, that may help your immediate future, but what's important is your inner drive to work hard. Below is a great quote that sums up being a better person.

"Doing the right thing isn't always easy, but it's always right."

———

When writing any letter, consider what you'd like to accomplish. Most of the notes I've written are based on specific themes. The one listed above is more about personal growth, but frequently during the year, the content will be academic, especially when students benefit from focusing on specific skills necessary for mastery. For example, suppose you were going to compose a letter after a test. Consider writing about those habits that would improve academic performance.

I can't overstate the importance of discussing what's written. Be sure to give examples that back up your letter. Students at any grade level need to see and hear specific ways to improve. A combination of writing, speaking, and showing is better than just one option.

I currently write letters or short notes about four to five times a semester. That may be too many for you. That's okay; you'll figure things out after you hand students your first one. I recommend an opening letter and a closing summation of the year. In this way, you've gotten off to a great start and finished with some positive words to leave them with.

One quick addition. If you are more of a video person, adding or substituting a video is a powerful tool for connecting with students and their parents. A video readily available to students can reinforce a positive message. It also allows parents to hear and see the personal connection you're attempting to make with their child. The initial time spent recording might seem long, but you'll master the skill quickly. The authentic results you're building are more than worth it. Ultimately, the students will respond enthusiastically, and you'll have many smiles and moments of joy.

You can do it:

1. How does your syllabus/opening letter or video cover details other than solely academic goals?
2. What written communication do you use to provide feedback on how students perform during the year?

Get going:

1. At the beginning of the year or in the first few weeks of school, write a brief (one-page) letter to students to update them on their progress or as an introduction to the class. You can also use a video if that suits your style.
2. Have students write their letters containing ideas they believe are essential for success in and out of school. For those who teach younger grades, the focus can be on keywords they think are crucial. Videos are also fun and exciting for all grades.

Notes

Section Three

Mirror Mirror

I mentioned in "Finding Your Go-To" that one of mine is post-it notes. They are also one of the backbones of how this section came to be. I'd always jot down notes before, during, and after class. By the end of each week, there would be scribbles and piles all over the place. So much so that I was forced to start putting them into Google docs to avoid more clutter than I usually had on my desk. There would be posts like:

- What was I thinking of during that lesson?
- Loved how kids chatted today with no prompting.
- Way off on that assessment today.
- Never play that song again!
- Q of the day caused lots of cheerful chatter.

- Peanut Butter is a fat source!
- Great Qs on relationships and avoiding toxicity.

Mirror/mirror is all about how we look at our practice. We should reflect daily, weekly, and yearly. For example, I'm sure many people in education were excited for the 20/21 year to end (given Covid and the lockdowns) and hopeful for a return to normalcy for 21/22. Sure, that is a broad way of reflecting and a more global view of education. But it still gets us thinking about our careers.

As I was writing the chapters for this part of the book, I understood (partly thanks to K.B.) that I needed to stop writing. She'd say, "Shap, stop! That's for another book." She was right. The art of reflection could easily encompass an entire book about teaching and learning. Thinking about our practice and habits is crucial to evaluating our successes and areas needed for growth. It's also vital for student growth, mastery, and overall success.

Reflection must be a questioning practice. If all we do is think everything is perfect or horrible, we never question our teaching. In both instances, we can become complacent in whatever role we have in education. Please know it is challenging for many in our field to look in that teaching mirror. Your focus should be centered on the great things you make happen each day and the minor adjustments that will help you and your school.

• CHAPTER 28 •
What Will I Try?

> " *Just because you haven't found your talent*
> *it doesn't mean you don't have one.*"
>
> — Kermit the Frog

As much as I hate to admit it, age has taken its toll on me. Taking pride in exercise and wellness was one reason I became a health and physical education teacher. Either fortunately or not, I've never been willing to accept that I can't do the same things at fifty-seven that I could at twenty-three. However, I learned this during a local Health and Physical Education convention.

Because I'd spent much of my time either presenting or participating in professional development sessions, my itch to do something physical was a great idea. As luck would have it (or so I thought), a "jump rope" exhibition attracted my attention. I've had many students jump rope at school and thought I'd learn a few new tricks. The team presenting was a group of exceptional younger students with tremendous skills. They demonstrated various stunts to the oohs and ahhs of the spectators. Following their performance, we were allowed to experiment. In the middle of trying a new trick (a push-up and skip), I landed with a thud on my big toe. Of course, since my shoe was untied (idiot move on my part), I limped for the next day and a half and took some razzing about it. It was all good fun, and more importantly, it helped me to think about trying new things and how that mindset translates to teaching.

Whether new to the field, or a veteran teacher, a person's willingness to try ideas is a big part of mastering our craft. It's impossible to keep doing the same things year after year without growing stagnant and boring your students to death. You'll either embrace the "trying-new-things" way of thinking, or it will be forced upon you. I encourage the former for many reasons. Having a teachable, innovative mindset can pave the way to successful teaching.

What I will try is all about . . .

Building connections with others - Whether it's planned professional development or a quick sharing of ideas, connecting at any level is an incredible way to improve a school's collegial culture. I've witnessed and been involved in many instances where colleagues learned from each other when it wasn't planned. Sharing with our peers promotes a sense of pride, ownership, and a collective spirit. Even if this were the only perk, it would be worth it.

Stoking creative teaching - About thirty minutes before starting this chapter, a colleague encouraged me to try advanced Google techniques. During the process, I experienced that "wow! moment" when we know something good will come from our hard work. Sure enough, students were challenged and excited to try what I learned. Creative teaching is all about growing, sharing, and trying new things. One caveat, try to avoid biting off more than you can chew. Even those initial small steps will foster academic excellence.

Promoting reflection on our practice - Considering the length of a school year, it's easy to only stick with lessons that have worked before. While I'd never advocate a "new for the sake of it" attitude, we want to avoid becoming complacent. Having a "what-will-I-try" mantra forces reflection upon us. Similarly, when you engage in new teaching, a powerful brain connection shapes your future ideas and provides positive feedback to our students.

Helping students to try new things - Students will model what they see, hear, and learn. If we always do the same activities or fear change, our students will do that too. Encouraging our students to step out of their comfort zones through our risk-taking will pay huge dividends, especially if we start with smaller projects that are sure to be successful.

Trying to master skills you didn't know you had - I hopped on the technology train about twelve years ago. I won't lie; learning new skills and tools wasn't easy. There were moments of stress and frustration. But that work spurred growth and the chance for students to utilize skills long after that initial first lesson, even if it wasn't perfect.

Initially, it might seem daunting when you think about what you will try. With practice and perseverance, you, your colleagues, and, most importantly, your students will see the growth that may have seemed unreachable before they took those risks.

You can do it:

1. What new technique or skill have you tried over the past year?
2. How has your "what-will-I-try" attitude encouraged your students to try new skills or learning methods?

Get going:

1. Please speak to a colleague about something new they have used in class and try it.
2. Pass along one or more ideas that have helped to transform your class.

• CHAPTER 29 •

The Elephant in the Locker Room

 Take a deep breath, get present in the moment,

and ask yourself 'What is important this very second?'"

— Greg McKeown

Soon after I started teaching high school, I was presenting a lacrosse lesson with one of the veteran teachers in our department. After the lesson ended, we walked to the locker room and started debriefing how awesome the kids were and how well the lesson went. A minute or two into our conversation, a student who was not in the class started slamming on the door, using language I won't repeat. It was shocking because we had just finished a great class.

Being new to the school, I wasn't prepared for this type of incident. While I'd seen crying or even angry elementary school students, this illustrated a new level of anger, especially from a seventeen-year-old boy.

When we opened the door, he stormed in and continued his tirade of profanity. He complained that another student had stolen his wallet and that he'd kill the thief if he found out who it was. Instead of yelling and screaming, my colleague moved away and reassuringly said, "It's okay. We'll find out who took your wallet. Try to calm down a little bit, so we can figure out exactly what happened." The student calmed down slightly but continued cursing. Once again, without losing his cool, my colleague politely asked him not to swear and remember that we were trying to help. After about five minutes of back and forth, we sat the student down and went over the steps necessary to find his wallet.

When the situation finally de-escalated, and we were alone, I asked my colleague, "How could you stay so calm when the student was upset and borderline violent?" He said, "Craig, he wasn't mad at me. He was upset about somebody taking his wallet. I tried not to take his anger personally but focused on finding a solution to the problem. His emotions were running wild, and the worst thing I could do was let mine do the same thing. Now you have two angry men instead of just one."

Looking back on what I learned that day, I still think long and hard about my colleague's calm demeanor when it would have been much easier to mirror the student's. Our ability to step back and analyze situations is necessary for reflection and classroom mastery. The average teacher is in the classroom about 180 to 190 days a year. There will be some moments to test your patience and fortitude. I started teaching with a full head of hair and lost most of it during the first fifteen years!

Keep in mind, though, that maintaining a sense of calm and low stress can be challenging. Even after seeing my colleague show restraint, I lost my cool with a student with whom I'd built a solid relationship.

Dominic always came into my health class before going into the locker room for the gym. I'd had him in health class the previous year, and we built a positive connection of respect. On this particular day, he came into the room, and one of the boys in the back made a negative comment. In turn, Dominic responded with a few choice words. Instead of staying calm, I got furious and told him to leave my room immediately. He said, "I'm sorry, Shap." I responded, "I don't care. Leave the room now. This language is inappropriate, and if you can't be respectful, then I'd prefer you not visit." He left my room, with my blood pressure through the roof. While that incident didn't have a lasting negative impact on our relationship, I felt awful about how I kicked him out and that I'd shown the other students in my class exactly how *not* to react to a situation.

I mention this incident because even though I'd learned about staying composed under stress from the locker room incident, it didn't matter.

Simply put, there are times when we forget how to keep our "mentality of a rider." It takes tons of practice and a desire for change to learn the art of staying calm under duress. The rider and elephant theme comes from the excellent book, *Switch* by authors Chip and Dan Heath. They share a superb example of a person riding an elephant. Even though the person is much smaller than the elephant, they can maintain control if they are rational and under control.

On the other hand, if the rider loses control, the elephant may go on a rampage. In my opening to this chapter, my colleague maintained his rider focus and did not let the situation (elephant) get out of control. I understood it, but I didn't apply it to Dominic.

To emphasize this, I also recommend another source. In his article "Five Ways to Be a Calmer Teacher," author Michael Linsin mentions the concept of "decide." He states, "Maintaining a calm attitude throughout your teaching day is a choice you make *before* your students arrive. So every day, sometime before the morning bell, give yourself a moment of peace to sit quietly at your desk. Take a few deep breaths and relax in your chair. Now decide that no matter what happens that day, no matter how crazy or how alarming, you will not lose your composure. And guess what? You won't."

I love that Linsin mentions using the same techniques every day. The habits of staying calm and rational with our thoughts and actions directly correlate to how students react in our classes and schools. Being able to demonstrate composure shows students that we are willing to see beyond one incident to the bigger picture. This action models a high level of professionalism and self-control, something we want our students to emulate. Everyone makes mistakes; that's part of teaching. While I wish I had reacted more wisely with Dominic, many students understood my anger and appreciated my honest response. It was because strong relationships were already established that this was a teachable moment instead of a permanently negative one.

In those times when you cannot try the techniques above, another great tool is applying the "10-second rule" before allowing emotions to run wild. I've deliberately waited ten seconds before speaking or acting when under pressure, and it's made a difference. Again, students will learn from our modeling, and when we apply these principles, you'll even be able to explain how it's helped you gather your thoughts.

As we close this chapter, please be aware of our hot-button issues. Whether it's a student coming late to class, phone usage, not working hard, or a host of concerns, being cognizant of what influences our actions becomes much easier if we reflect positively on our core values of relationship building.

You can do it:

1. Think about a situation where you lost your composure and wished you would have handled a situation differently. What good may have come from this if you had acted calmly?
2. How do you stay calm and positive when a complex conflict arises?

Get going:

1. Give students at least ten seconds to respond when doing verbal questioning and answering with students.
2. Discuss and analyze with students how they react when challenging situations arise. Make list or poster of what was mentioned. This will keep it fresh in their minds.

· CHAPTER 30 ·
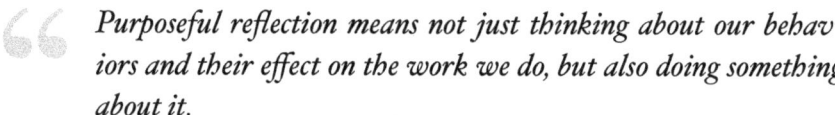
LOOK IN THE MIRROR

> *Purposeful reflection means not just thinking about our behaviors and their effect on the work we do, but also doing something about it.*
>
> *'What am I going to do differently to meet student needs?'"*
>
> — Tony Frontier

On most days after school, I'm lucky enough to have students and athletes visiting me to chat about their day, discuss life issues, and generally unwind from a hectic day. While many are light-hearted, sometimes a talk will leave a lasting impression. November of 2018 was one such moment. One of the boys I coached for Cross Country stopped in. I could tell from his body language that he was upset about something. He mentioned a negative situation, and we discussed how taking a few minutes to reflect might be the best way to avoid a repeat situation. As our conversation ended, he mentioned how he appreciated our time together and learned some valuable lessons. In retrospect, that conversation helped me look at what parts of my teaching were working, how I could adjust my lessons to reach more students, and why the process of looking in the mirror is ever-changing.

Reflection is crucial to learning, promoting academic success, and developing our practice. Our brains remember and forget things relatively quickly, but by consistently reflecting on what we've done and its impact on others, we can fine-tune areas that may need improvement. The concept seems relatively simple, but reflection is complicated for many, myself included. It can be challenging to know *what* to reflect on, *how to implement* change, and *why* adjustments may be necessary even after the process is in action. Hopefully, the guidelines below will clarify a few valuable methods you can start trying today.

The What - This is the most challenging facet of the reflection process. Do we try to reflect on every class, lesson, day, week, etc.? Do we make wholesale changes to our assessments and teaching practices? There isn't any clear-cut way to answer those questions. The methods that work for one person might be too much or too little for another. My best suggestion, though, is to start simple. A single class lesson, a segment of that lesson, or even just the beginning or end of class is much more manageable than thinking about a significant unit change.

By picking one small area you know can be addressed, it becomes much easier to move forward and feel successful. I use those trusty post-it notes, a Google doc, or a lesson outline book to quickly jot down my impressions of an activity or lesson for later reflection. By picking a small part of your teaching day or a particular lesson as an entry point, you'll usually have at least a few moments to collect your thoughts when school ends. Plus, you won't be so overwhelmed with a hundred details that you'll "blow it off" until later. Since the results are fresh in your mind, and you've made notes of them, it's much more practical and valuable to think about "why" things did or didn't work than to wait days or weeks. Also, the end of the day brings a natural closure to classes.

The How - I mentioned in "UBD," an earlier chapter, that our brains could only process so much information simultaneously. From experience, I recommend you start with an obvious purpose. Beginning the "how" with something you know can be completed will allow you to adjust and expand on ideas as you get comfortable. For instance, perhaps you've just started "exit tickets" to bring closure to a great lesson. By reflecting on those exit tickets, the "***how***" can I make them more effective may be as simple as changing a few minor details, adding a "hook" to make things even more engaging, or even sometimes keeping things the same. Because it's a daily activity, possible changes are simple. More importantly, the transition to more complex challenges may not seem daunting since you've succeeded.

Another example is when you assess students with a test or quiz. Since you've already figured out the basics of reflective practice, it becomes second nature to try new things. Because these areas of instruction often carry more weight and usually stress kids out way too much, you'll be able to provide many options that may reduce their anxiety. How we address poor results or success is critical. In both instances, our "how" is grounded in improved academic achievement. Always keep in mind that you're trying to promote success.

The Why - Why we reflect should be grounded in equity, diversity, enjoyment, relationships, and assessment of students. This should be occurring on an even playing field while making your class a safe space for all students. It shouldn't take long to see how each student learns differently. Why we reflect is not a one-size-fits-all approach. Every teacher will find a way to build lessons into their classroom. Reflection is an ongoing, sometimes challenging practice. But it's worth it.

From the moment students walk into our rooms, our willingness to recognize and make instructional changes is the cornerstone of meaningful teaching. When we look in the mirror, a bright, optimistic vision should be what we see.

———

Zoe's Letter

Having Mr. Shapiro as a teacher shattered everything I have learned about education. I was taking all honors courses and was not used to being mixed with "A" track kids. So it was safe to say that I was not looking forward to learning about sex and drugs with them. But what I learned from that class was much more than that. Mr. Shapiro taught me things that have changed who I am, some I did not realize until I left the class.

The biggest thing significantly different from all my other learning experiences was the amount of personalization Mr.Shapiro included. Beyond getting everyone to participate in class discussions (which before I had never bothered to do), he emphasized that every student was different. Instead of being told something had to be three paragraphs or a page long, Mr.Shapiro told us to do "as much as we thought was our best." He understood that some students could get their point across in one paragraph, whereas others liked to use two or three.

After leaving his classroom, I noticed a difference in how I think and act. I have started to take fitness more seriously and become a more engaged student. I am no longer afraid to make comments in class. I ask questions frequently with no shame of being thought of as dumb. Most importantly, I have started to look at the world with bright eyes. All of these things have made me a better student and a better person.

Zoe Khodak

Class of 2019

———

You can do it:

1. How do you currently use reflection in your class?
2. How are students given chances to reflect on their progress in your class?

Get going:

1. Reflect on one particular lesson, day, or activity you recently taught.
2. Consider how your "what, how, and why" may improve instruction.

· CHAPTER 31 ·

Be in the Moment

Changing lives, one light bulb moment at a time!"

— Rachel Parrott

I am a big fan of Twitter - @Shapiro_WTHS - #teachpos (every Sunday at 7:30 p.m. EST with a fantastic, growing group of educators) and @Positively_Well. So much so that I had to promise my wife that I'd avoid tweeting on a recent vacation. I tried my best and generally succeeded, with only a slight tweet withdrawal. When we arrived home, I immediately hopped on Twitter to find a friend's post. He shared articles on students being curious, the changing nature of learning, and suggestions on improving attentiveness.

As my wife and I drove to pick up our dogs from the kennel, I shared what the reading stated, especially how different education looks from decades ago. We volleyed ideas about technology, lecturing, play, etc. My wife repeated a common phrase to me during that conversation: "Be in the moment!"

Frankly, it connects naturally to the whole "teachable moment" idea. No doubt, you've heard that term hundreds of times. It's one of the most overused phrases and underutilized concepts. A teachable moment is not during that one evaluation from a supervisor. Instead, think about a typical school year; there are thousands of times when we can "be in the moment," mainly because they often occur with no planning.

So what is "being in the moment?" It is the willingness to provide students with intellectual, emotional, social, and physical benefits without a plan. It adjusts spontaneously to kids' learning, interests, and even problems. Whether by necessity or want, being willing to teach "on the spot" is part of effective instruction. Being in the moment acknowledges that not every minute can be planned. Sometimes those quick adaptations will enhance your instruction, helping your students in ways you didn't envision.

Education has long followed the same structure because it's familiar and comfortable—almost born from necessity. Even if this isn't inherently wrong, it can quickly push us to be so cautious that in-the-moment instruction can be daunting. That said, the intrinsic value of capturing a student's interest and motivation when an unplanned occurrence arises is a valuable tool for improving academic growth and the classroom climate.

I realize that some may be cynical about how often being in the moment matters or if it destroys a class's flow. To be clear, I'm not suggesting seeking out moments just for the sake of it. Instead, be willing to accept that sometimes moments will happen without planning. They will promote socialization, show students you are adaptable, and provide meaningful leadership skills to students. Also, these moments are usually short interjections to get us and our students to reflect. When I think back to many of the unique moments that have become special, most have been a quick laugh, a short story, a tip on life, or even something I didn't want to pass over for fear of forgetting about it later. Sure, some have turned into lessons that students talked about at the end of the year, but that makes them even more special.

Spontaneity doesn't just happen. The teacher in the room allows it to occur. Instructional settings that are solely teacher driven suffocate these opportunities. But those classrooms that are dynamic spaces with many interactions foster creative learning. Below are some helpful tips.

- Ask questions encouraging students to discuss a topic instead of just providing "the right answer."
- Design lessons that contain content, dialogue, writing, and other forms of communication.
- Consistently use what they've learned and connect that learning with "real-world experiences." Allow students to collaborate and think deeply about learning and how they value the content. I love to do a word of the day. Sometimes it's content-related, but just as frequently, it might be something they've never heard of, like "negation," which I had to look up after my wife mentioned the word!
- Use prompts that provide a message that resonates with students. It can be the classroom decoration or setting, the clothes you wear, the music playing, a holiday or birthday celebration, or any other powerful idea that educators regularly use to inspire students.
- Keep kids guessing. Even though a routine is of great value, students spend much of their day sitting in chairs, inside a building, and not moving. In pleasant weather, get students outside for a lesson. The results are positive. Even singing a song, dancing in class, playing a quick game, or breaking up the monotony of study will do wonders for instruction flow.

A combination of planning and intuitive teaching can captivate your class. The best thing is the connections you'll build with students. I encourage you to start small. Shake hands, tell a joke, give a sticker, play a song, go for a walk, dress up, or do something that takes little preparation time. Once you see the success of your actions, you'll be inspired to try new things.

You can do it:

1. How rigidly do you hold on to your daily plan if something is not working?
2. What spontaneous "risks" have you taken to benefit your teaching and students?

Get going:

1. Think about one of the ideas mentioned above. Give it a try, and then have students give feedback.
2. Whether transitioning between units or lessons, try a new game, lesson, brain-break, or anything unique and different.

CHAPTER 32
YOUR BEST

"So often we think that our best isn't good enough when in reality our best is our best."

I just finished another one of the many great conversations with my good friend and fantastic colleague, Dave Fries. I mentioned Dave earlier in the book with one of his quotes about the variables of teaching. We were quickly (for us, fast is 30 minutes) discussing the challenges of education in a Covid-19 world and comparing it to past years when all kids were in school. As the conversation came to a close, I recall he mentioned: "I'm still providing a great education, but I can't just magically jump through the screen into their house." His quote resonated with me deeply, as I had been thinking if I was genuinely giving my best to our students.

Our class was ending our fitness/nutrition unit. We'd spent five days online going over many key terms, and I was happy to move on from the "peanut butter is not mainly a protein source" conversation. As had been a frequent occurrence in class, I'd call on students, play games to check for understanding, do various tricks to ensure they were alive behind the icon, and check in for any questions. When I called a few students, some quickly got the answers, which was a great start. Then things went downhill! Multiple students either didn't answer, said, "sorry, Shap, I wasn't listening," or got the answer wrong. I paused and kept my composure, mentioning that I wasn't angry but just a little frustrated that we'd covered this so many times. As the class ended, I stopped for a minute to ponder the lesson, students not focusing, and teaching in such a unique environment. After jotting down some notes and laughing to myself for getting frustrated, I realized I'd given my best effort. While everyone didn't fully understand everything, it wasn't from a lack of passion, energy, and enthusiasm. Sure, in retrospect, I could have done things a little differently. But in some instances, that's self-defeating. We must be willing to accept that our best is our best.

Part numbers, part feel - As a person who enjoys looking at data, it's easy to use just numbers to guide your best instruction. If we give a quiz and twenty out of twenty students get A's, there is a tendency to think things went well. While that's a great starting point, our best teaching goes beyond just that quick data point. When assessing students beyond just one measure, you'll learn when the class or a student gets it and when they don't. It won't happen on your first day of teaching, but over time, you'll figure out the cues to see if mastery has occurred. Because a few students may struggle doesn't mean your effort is lacking. I'm also not suggesting we forget about those students who might need more help. A great way to see if your original thoughts of academic success were correct is to wait a few weeks and assess the class again. If the results are mostly the same, or even better, thank you for doing your best.

When in doubt, ask - If I had a dollar for each time I've asked, "does anyone have any questions," I'd be a millionaire, and I'm not kidding. So many times, we ask if students have questions or if they understand the material. That's just part of good teaching. Students may not say anything for various reasons; sometimes, none relate to whether they truly understand the material. Students have been programmed to be compliant. There are many games and activities to get them to ask for help. Even more important is trying a relaxed approach. Sometimes it's as simple as backing off, giving them a moment to chill, and trying something new. I was amazed when I first tried this. It initially caught the class off-guard, but in a short time, great questions started and helped those hesitant students to see it wasn't so bad.

Let things sink in - Please let things sink in! When speaking with other educators, I often hear how easy it becomes to harp on a lesson that didn't go perfectly, a class that struggled, or something that got them stressed. In reality, we are humans, not robots. From time to time, a class will go poorly, or the school day's daily grind wears on us. If we take even a few minutes to let things sink in and realize that we are doing our best, the change will be positive.

Throughout three-plus decades of being in the classroom, I've known many leaders, support staff, and teachers who've consistently raised the bar of being better each day. While I admire this immensely, please don't let it cause an "I"m not good enough" attitude when things don't go as planned. Try to avoid thinking that your best isn't good enough. Focus on the great things you do, and remember that your best is enough to improve students' lives.

You can do it:

1. Have you considered the incredible impact your best effort has on students? If yes, how does that affect your teaching?
2. How can you help students to see that their best effort will translate to improved learning?

Get going:

1. Take a few moments after a unit, test, or major assignment and ask students if something you did helped them learn the material and what it was.
2. After completing number one, ask students to reflect on if they did their best work and how that might have impacted learning and enjoyment of the class.

• CHAPTER 33 •

When Gab is not a Gift

 What I love most about my classroom is who I share it with."

— Unknown

Having started teaching in the lower grades, I was always impressed with how enthusiastic younger students loved answering questions or giving feedback. You get many hands raised simultaneously, with lots of oohs and ahhs. Even though most of those sounds are indistinguishable from simple noises, it often beats the upper grades. Case in point: having just finished a quiz in health class, I asked students to reflect on what they could improve upon. In typical fashion, most did a combination of looking down at their desk, sitting on their hands, or the occasional stare that's code for "Shap, can you just move on, please." Luckily, every once in a while, a student will strike a chord that resonates. After listening to a few semi-forced responses, one answer hit the target: "Shap, I love your positivity, energy, and caring attitude, but no disrespect, you talk way too much." I laughed, and the class did as well (with lots of head nodding). That brief conversation helped me to take a serious look at my instructional techniques.

After so many years of teaching, coaching, and presenting, I find speaking enjoyable. Unfortunately, that comfort has sometimes led me to get caught up in my voice instead of being a great listener and observer. Many teachers and people who work with kids are natural talkers. We want our voices to be heard so that students can be successful in class, even when it is better to listen and watch. Tied to this issue is the challenge of examining how often we "have the last word," as if talking were a competitive sport. Because of this, I've learned to ramp up activities that advance students' voices, participation, and conversations rather than just my own. Body language can tell a great deal, and when students look glassy-eyed, with drool coming from their mouths, it's time to be quiet and let the students take charge.

If you happen to have the gift of gab, it may be time to implement strategies that focus more on student interaction than teacher talk. There is no magical formula for this type of instruction. Many teachers have their ways of promoting class collaboration. Designing plans that compel kids to get involved, allowing you to listen more intently and then interject when the time is right, is a great start. Here are some practical ways to gab less and listen more.

Get them going quickly. Many of us use pre-class activities to introduce a topic, ask a question, or provide some time to get familiar with our class. This is a fantastic idea, as long as you explain only some details. We want to avoid thirty minutes of instruction and five minutes of student engagement. A simple solution is to keep the directions simple. A short video, questions on a board, or any other exciting activity will nicely accomplish this goal. Once students get going, avoid, at all costs, frequently interrupting to interject.

When giving feedback, keep it relevant to your teaching, and move on.

Google Apps and Others are Awesome - Many unique applications exist to engage students, with more coming every year. Every teacher should at least try the various applications from Google. Tools like Docs, Slides, Forms, Sites, etc., can bring something collaborative to your class. Plus, you can keep directions short by using writing prompts as a guide. Of course, many technology applications are also great options. While I like Padlet, Flipgrid, Go Formative, GiveThx, and Canva, I'm sure there will be many more apps when you read this chapter. By stressing the importance of empowering students, you'll spend much less time talking to the entire class and more energy walking around (10,000 steps), interacting with small groups, and generally giving meaningful praise for the outstanding work that's being done.

Find avenues to let students teach each other. One of the best parts of small talk is the big actions that happen when students can work together. We know the power of collaborative learning. Seeing fantastic work done by small groups would have been impossible had we lectured the whole class. I've found that a blend of integrating real-life experiences with those of your students is a practical starting point to raise the engagement scale. It may even encourage those generally more quiet students to get involved.

Honor the value of time. If you still need help with talking too much, and none of the other suggestions help, you can try this trick. Set a timer for yourself. I needed reminders when I first started chatting less and engaging kids more. Since students would always have phones in class, I asked one to set her phone to ten minutes. She would signal me if I were close to running out of time. We'd take a little break, get up, and stretch, or I'd provide the class with a discussion question to work on. This forced me to be quiet. In our profession, time moves fast. Before we know it, the class is over! Setting time parameters for yourself will effectively create a positive flow to the class.

A passionate, enthusiastic, empowering, and knowledgeable presenter makes learning authentic. The same holds for our students. The balance between learning to talk just enough and not too much will only happen after a while. I still deal with this issue, but it's gotten better. If you're lucky, you may not ever deal with this problem. But if you do, learning brevity will be the difference between having students hang on to your every word and those that hit their heads on the desk from sleeping.

You can do it:

1. How many minutes or the percentage of time do you spend talking during a class period? What about your students?
2. Do your students tell you the lessons they most enjoy? Is there a correlation between how much talking you're doing and how much they enjoy the class?

Get going:

1. Use one of the ideas listed in this chapter to curb your talking and promote student engagement.
2. Have an activity where each student times and records how much talking they do during a group activity. Avoid making things a competition; instead, discuss the observations they learned.

• CHAPTER 34 •

Don't Run Out of Gas

(With permission from Michael Sander)

 Don't be upset by the results you didn't get with the work you didn't do."

— Unknown

When you've taught for a while, the fortunate experience of getting to know dedicated educators is another fantastic perk of being in education. Since starting as a substitute teacher in 1988, I've been blessed to create friendships and share many unforgettable moments, along with learning critical tips that have shaped my teaching. Some have happened on purpose, but most occurred as a conversation while visiting a colleague's class. Chatting with your peers is a win/win and shouldn't just happen solely during a faculty meeting. This chapter and its relevance to long-term teaching success would have never happened if I hadn't walked into a friend's room and sat down.

Frequently during the year, my good friend and former social studies teacher Mick Sander would ask me to come into his class and do a current event on a Friday. Even though our disciplines weren't explicitly related, we always shared the common goals of learning new things and never being afraid to take risks. While Mick and I always appreciated the time teaching together, coming into a co-worker's room can be challenging. But Mick always welcomed me, and it was the utmost compliment that he allowed his class to learn from me. Thank you, Mick, for the chance to share some fantastic times with you and your students.

Along with Mick, I'd often visit my coaching colleague, Mr. Rob Mulville. We'd always have great conversations, and Rob is a fantastic educator. On one particular occasion, Rob and I were chatting about how to motivate athletes best. Luckily, Mick strolled in as I was babbling along. (He probably had some sensory intuition about these kinds of topics. Or maybe he saw me enter the room and tried to save Rob.) After hearing bits and pieces of our dialogue, Mick said,

"Do you guys know the *GAS Gap* principle?"

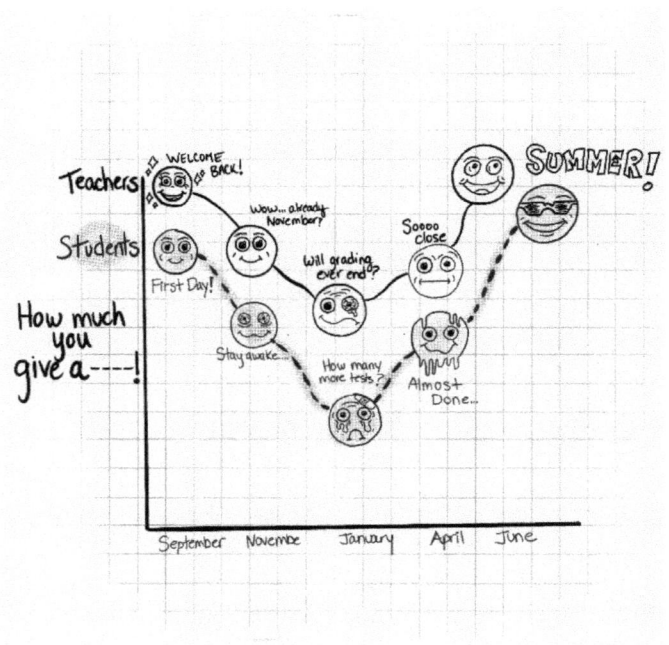

Rob mentioned that Mick had brought it up before, but he couldn't remember it clearly. I said, "No, I have no idea what you're speaking about."

Mick proceeded to draw an X and Y graph on the board, with my recollection being the X and Y-Axis representing teachers/students and the X-axis representing the time of year. At this point, I still had no clue what he was thinking, but after listening to and watching Mick, the brief conversation had a lasting influence on the school year and staying motivated.

After drawing the axis on the board, Mick mentioned that the "GAS" in *GAS Gap* stands for "Give A Sh--." Rob and I started to laugh because who even comes up with a name like that? If you knew Mick, it's him to a tee.

Mick explained that you want it to be equal along both axis points. From the beginning of the year to the end, the goal is to have both the students and teachers at high levels of giving a sh--. Of course, he said, what usually happens is that it's easy for everyone to be feeling good in the very beginning. We're excited to greet our students; many kids don't know us and are still figuring things out. As the year progresses, though, especially during the holiday season and later in the year, there is a tendency for student interest to drop significantly and a teacher's level also to plummet. The three of us debated and discussed the merits of the *GAS Gap* and how to best keep it at the highest levels for students and staff. I don't recall the whole dialogue, but I remember our strong inclination that teachers must lead by example. As our conversation ended, I started to think about my *GAS Gap* and how it related to what we'd just discussed.

I've never met any person in education who doesn't look forward to the holiday break and summer. I love my job, but the mid-year break offers a time to recharge and spend quality moments with the family. Summer vacation is the opportunity to reflect on the year, spend time away, and even learn new ideas before the next school year starts. I've always told students that we should all treasure the breaks in the school year. They are a necessary way to stay motivated.

With the above out of the way, the most straightforward advice on the *GAS Gap* is that students will follow our lead. Students usually follow suit when we come in excited about the new school year. Just as when May comes, we look forward to family time, beaches, and simply a break from the school routine. There is absolutely nothing wrong with that. It's real!

On the other hand, senioritis has that name for a reason. Whoever came up with that name experienced firsthand the power of April, May, and June. My point is that we are role models for students and other faculty members. Avoiding the *GAS Gap* entails a certain level of Robert De Niro and Meryl Streep showmanship. Teaching with a passion existed when the beginning of the year started and should continue no matter the month. While there aren't any special magic tricks to help cure the ills of the *GAS Gap*, here are some easy ways to at least be cognizant of our fuel tank.

Stay positive - Staying positive isn't some fancy technique or catchy lesson that students will "ooh and ahh" over. It's a mindset and much more powerful. We can't deny the power of showing a happy face and bringing an inspired attitude to class daily. While for some, this comes naturally, others have to focus on the good things that happen—staying positive and working hard until the end. If that's a struggle, remember that your attitude will contribute to better academic achievement, fewer discipline issues, and higher student morale.

Avoid the noise - We've all been in those situations where colleagues complain about something kid-related. I've done that, and I regret it. But there is a vast difference between being a good colleague and listening and being a doormat for negativity. We owe it to ourselves and our students to stay away from those whose only message is "I can't wait to retire. I can't wait for the summer. I can't wait to be done with this year!" This can be tough, especially involving people you speak with daily, but there is no real benefit to enabling that language and behavior.

Mix it up - Nothing will make the year seem like it's dragging on than never deviating from a lesson. The structure is fantastic and truly necessary for all kids. But we all need some sense of "newness" to keep things exciting and fun. I'm not suggesting that anyone change how you teach because of the month of the year. Instead, it's about being flexible enough with your teaching to realize the value of surprising students.

Power up your class - We want students to work hard and be motivated until the last day of school. In the past, I'd say, "Hey, everyone, let's focus on doing our best up until the end." Yes, that would work for some kids. But most teens would nod or say, "We got you!" Then, of course, it would be the same *GAS Gap* that happened before. I read about "powering up" your class a few years ago. It was so simple that I just shrugged it off. But with nothing changing, I figured, let's give it a go. Powering up is merely bringing a powerful voice and actions to your expectations. At first, when I'd say, "Everyone, are you ready to POWER-UP our class," the students would stare at me like I was from another planet. Then I'd ask again, and, finally, they'd get the message. Powering up is about raising our energy and motivation to keep students from losing focus. The phrase might make them laugh, but it will also inspire them to try harder.

When I first heard of the *GAS Gap from Mick*, it made me smile. Then I realized how sad it was that we'd be talking about teachers and students not caring as much later in the year as they did when it started. While I thought the message was always clear to keep working hard, I also understood that it's so easy for many of us not to promote that Gas Gap thinking. An excellent question for students is to ask them on June 1st, "What's the difference between September 1st and June 1st?" You'll get an array of answers, but no matter what students say, you can always answer, "In September, you started good, now it's June, and you're going to finish off great!"

You can do it:

1. How do you keep all your students motivated throughout the year?
2. How do you keep *yourself* from "running out of GAS" as the year progresses?

Get going:

1. Before the holiday breaks and later in the year, try something new and exciting that you've never done before.
2. Give students choices either before a holiday or as the year progresses. Keep them purposeful and engaging.

https://nittany1991.wordpress.com/2020/06/18/the-gas-gap/

· CHAPTER 35 ·

Strengths are Key - A Few Weaknesses As Well

 Change will not come if we wait for some other person or if we wait for some other time.

We are the ones we've been waiting for. We are the change that we seek."

— Barack Obama

As our school year closes, staff are given a log-out sheet to turn in as we look forward to summer. It has the typical items of the phone number, address, any changes to the room, and making sure that all materials are cleared from the walls and desk. Most of these are easy, but desk cleaning is a daunting task for me. I'd found some older pictures to represent the clutter visually. Unfortunately, I deleted them out of embarrassment!

As educators, we all have specific skill sets and qualities that make us unique to students. Keeping my desk clean isn't one of them. Hopefully, for students, my love of teaching and wellness will make up for the mess. While it may be hard to identify your strengths and weaknesses when your career starts, you'll most definitely figure them out as the years pass. This seemingly simple liability is all about hating to throw things out. My inherent fear is that the one paper or email I delete will be needed in an emergency. Of course, this is incredibly silly. There is no real reason to keep a quiz from five years ago or 32,121 emails from 2017. But I've been blessed and cursed to sometimes share my room with an OCD colleague who is fantastic. I hope she reads this. She will shake her head and laugh hysterically!

Whatever your weakness is, the first step in fixing it is realizing that it might be detrimental to your performance and even cause you stress. Sure, you will have to be vigilant; my desk looks great at the end of the year when I have to clean it. Within one month of the next school year, it has post-it notes, letters, papers, cans of chicken breast, and other items. Luckily, that clutter is obvious, so it's not hard to be motivated enough to clean it up. Maybe you have less easily seen or observed habits like my "gift of gab" discussed earlier. Small steps, like reflection and persistence, will help you get started on the right path. Both good and bad habits can be challenging to remove or cultivate. As in most changes, things aren't hopeless. With a few minor tweaks, you can make your strengths truly transformative and your weakness into a strength as well. Because this section is about reflection, we must consider and recognize our strengths and weaknesses. How are they impacting our attitudes about teaching/leading/supporting? How do they influence the learning that is happening with students? Again, my messy desk isn't usually affecting how students learn, but it is frustrating. This may have a carryover influence that I overlook. Here are some ways to improve those weaknesses and make those strengths shine.

Take a few minutes and think about your strengths and possible weaknesses. It's not uncommon for us to notice our strengths by choice or because it affirms how we want to feel about our teaching. Flaws can be harder to see. It becomes easy to figure it out by observing our practices and attitudes. Using the following questions can guide our thinking:

- Are your strengths helping students to enjoy learning?
- Is there a weakness that is influencing how students perform in class?
- Do our daily habits positively or negatively promote success for all kids?

Now that you've figured out your strengths and weaknesses, it's time to get going on them. I've always found that starting with a strength is what motivates me. You may feel differently. By starting with your strength(s), you realize it's something you already do well; making it even better feels good. On the other hand, improving or eliminating a weakness can feel liberating. Whichever way you choose to move forward, it's important not to overwhelm yourself. This is especially the case when it involves instructional techniques, for example, lesson planning and assessments. Those are both huge parts of teaching. Take them on slowly and with a purpose.

While focusing on strengths and weaknesses, try to see and ask students how they impact their learning. Through the years, I've learned that my strength in building relationships positively impacted my teaching. Plus, talking less (the gift of gab, a weakness) improved how students interacted with each other, helped the instructional flow, and strengthened my connections with students. You'll get the perk of making adjustments by seeing that they improve your teaching and student learning.

As hard as it may be, reaching out to your colleagues for guidance can help get the ball rolling. Sometimes they will validate your thoughts or maybe provide helpful tips that they've used to build positive habits. Of course, we never want this to turn into an "I do this better than you" that serves no purpose. The goals are about recognizing improvements you are trying to make and having pride in those things you already do well. We all have skills that are admirable and faults to admit. You and your students will benefit from the process by taking the time to address, improve, and implement positive changes to your instruction.

You can do it:

1. How do your strengths and weaknesses influence learning in your classroom or school?
2. How might you have students identify your teaching strengths and weaknesses?

Get going:

1. Pick one strength or challenge to work on over the next week or two.
2. Discuss with students their strengths and possible weaknesses. Then come up with a few strategies to either improve upon strengths or lessen liabilities.

• CHAPTER 36 •

WHAT'S *your* STYLE...

> *More important than the curriculum is the methods of teaching
> and the spirit in which the teaching is given."*
>
> — Bertrand Russell

I n the chapter "Dear Students," I mentioned my love of sharing a letter of tips with all students. It's a way to give them a festive send-off and get feedback about their thoughts on the class. As I was reading one of the responses, it struck me that some students had mentioned "your style" as a repeated comment. Thinking about my teaching style isn't something I'd done in the past. Luckily, reading about it from students made me think and reflect on my teaching.

We all have varied styles. No two educators are the same. Each of us brings different personalities and traits to our schools and classes. Thinking about our styles can be beneficial, though. It allows for a more in-depth look at our effectiveness and may reinforce excellence or promote ways to enhance our instructional approach. Before jumping into strategies for developing your style, let me share a few of mine. This isn't meant to be about what's good or bad. Instead, it's a starting point to think about your style.

- **Loud** - From my background as a coach and a health and physical education teacher, I've always had a loud voice. Even at home, my family will continuously remind me to stop yelling. It's been a work in progress. While most students won't say anything, I'll tone it down now that I know it might impact others.

- **Storyteller** - I'm still determining how I started with this teaching style. Most likely, it's from thinking back to teachers I enjoyed and remembering that I always loved when they told stories. I must be careful, though, since the chapter on talking too much is a constant reminder.
- **Flexible** - During my early college classes, my professors rigidly enumerated how to submit work, what happened if it was late, and how grades were assigned. Much of this felt subjective (which it is). On the other hand, being flexible makes life easier for our students and us. Being flexible contributes to opportunities that might only occur if we realize what is truly best for students.
- **Positive** - In section one, I mentioned that my promise for the year was to always come in happy and positive. While some might not think of that as a style, when students say that positivity is one thing they like about class, we can't negate that level of importance.
- **Chill** - Remembering my calculus class with Mrs. Gold, it always struck me how laid back and chilled she was. Her demeanor created a low-stress course. In retrospect, it led me to follow that same classroom style. Being chill tends to get students relaxed and comfortable. I'd like to think my teaching style directly reflects what made her class special.

Figuring out your style starts with the simple task of thinking about your style. Even if we reflect on our teaching, that's different from style analysis. Teaching reflection concerns lesson planning, assessments, data analysis, students' responses to our instruction, and so forth. Our style is more about our behaviors, language, and interactions with kids. While there is an overlap between the two, most teachers I've met during my career rarely mention their style.

Are you strict? Easy going? Open-minded? Funny? No matter your answers, getting those initial thoughts down on paper is enormous. We can only make a meaningful change if we first consider what connects with students and some possible hurdles our style creates. As I've mentioned in previous chapters, please avoid the desire to fix everything at once. It won't work. Baby steps are critical. Pick one style trait you know is attainable and build from that base. For example, from my list above, I am confident I can work on being a little less loud. That's something that will enhance the classroom. It's not an impossible task, and as long as I'm transparent with students, I know it will be better for everyone. Also, realize that just because you develop a particular style doesn't mean you won't have to keep working on it. I recently told my class that when I'm not excited to teach on certain days, I force myself to think about the "positive" promise I made.

Our teaching and leadership styles shape how students learn, how faculty think of school, and our behaviors, attitudes, and actions. Keep in the back of your mind the power style has on your students and others. Even the littlest change can make a big difference.

You can do it:

1. What are the benefits of thinking about your teaching style or leadership style?
2. What would your students say is your style?

Get going:

1. Whatever your role is, take a few minutes to jot down bullet points related to your style.
2. Ask students to describe or discuss their style of learning.

———

Owen Proctor Letter

Dear Mr. Shapiro

It's hard for me to describe your impact on me. Not just as a student but also as a person. You are more than just a teacher who comes to class daily to help his students. You enlighten people in all aspects of life. I could not have asked for a better teacher, and I could not be more thankful to have met you during my 10th-grade year as a sophomore. That particular year was rough, and I was not feeling very "well." But every day I had your class, it made me feel so much better, whether I showed it or not. Each day seeing a smile on your face and having you shake my hand brought happiness to your entire class. To me, that's how an actual teacher should be. You made learning fun, kept my attention, and turned my life around. I cannot thank you enough for all the good you have done.

Mr. Shapiro. Thank you!

Sincerely, Owen Procter

Class of 2018

• CHAPTER 37 •
I hated it... Now I LOVE it!

> *Your work is going to fill a large part of your life, and the only way to be truly satisfied is to do what you believe is great work. And the only way to do great work is to love what you do."*
>
> — Steve Jobs

L et's face it, one challenge in education is maintaining an optimistic attitude. Especially for those who have spent much of their adult life teaching, there may come a dry period where the well of "this is awesome" runs dry. While there isn't an exact solution to this issue, a colleague, Ed, is an excellent example of somebody who embraced the notion that "we can change" for the better.

I noticed Ed's transformation from a somewhat cynical educator who struggled to enjoy the classroom experience to one who found a new lease on teaching after returning from a sabbatical. Hopefully, you might understand his stance and be inspired by his story.

One day I'd stopped over to Ed's class to check in and see how he was doing. He had a class of students listening to music (a great choice) and was very engaged in the class. I asked him, "What happened? You're different!" He stated, "I realized there wasn't any way I could continue for another fifteen years if things didn't change. I took additional classes outside teaching and my content area during my sabbatical. I took a risk and realized that it was okay and essential to get out of my comfort zone. In the past, I was constantly worried about what I had to cover and what test was given, and I generally felt pressured to meet every deadline. Now, with lots of reflection, I enjoy teaching and recognize valuable moments aside from a specific lesson that's taught. Unfortunately, much of what's changed me isn't anything that we are formally taught. I hope to pass along some of the positive stuff to others." I was so inspired that my colleague found that positive change.

Being in education for three decades has given me plenty of opportunities to hear and see those who started out enjoying teaching and then, for many reasons, became cynical and miserable in the classroom.

While it's not given as much attention, there are many more situations like Ed's—where educators have rediscovered their mojo and love how exciting and rewarding teaching can be. We need to spend more time focusing on helping teachers ignite their passion than on every reason why somebody has given up in the classroom or education. There isn't a college course on enjoying your job, taking risks, and moving out of your comfort zone. Ed acknowledged that he had to do some serious soul-searching and reflection on his practice for change to happen. It's impossible to list and discuss all the possible ways to get that mojo. Hopefully, the four guidelines below may help.

♡ Find time for yourself! I'm the first to admit that I love my job. It's great spending time with exceptional students and colleagues. But I've also learned the importance of time for me. I tend to be a workaholic, so being wrapped up in work is easy. Over time, even the most exciting job can become draining when that's your sole focus. The time you spend on yourself must be for you. Whether it's a hobby, exercise, watching television, reading, etc., it can't involve work or anything related to your job. While you may think it's not a big deal, you'll be amazed at how refreshing and rejuvenating it is to have something to do other than work. Also, spending time thinking and doing other things helps create a natural balance between work and play. You'll feel ready to continue loving your job when the play is done.

♥ Reach out to others! A lurking danger in our profession is becoming stuck in our four walls and rarely coming out. That's a huge mistake.

Asking questions, sharing tips, and making positive connections are a big part of the "tribe" mentality. When they say, "it takes a village," that holds value in our field. Throughout the book, I've known many colleagues who impacted my teaching. This isn't accidental. Even if you are not naturally outgoing, taking some initial steps to reach out to others will pay dividends professionally and personally. Here are some quick ideas that will help:

- Go out in the halls and chat with your colleagues next to you. Between classes is a great way to interact with both kids and them.
- Share a positive comment about their class. It's a fantastic way to show that you care and are interested in working together.
- Promote an idea that's worked for you. Be careful to avoid coming on too strong with this, but mention in passing that you tried something in class that worked well and would love to share it if they are interested.
- If you happen to have the same prep period (if you have them), eating lunch together is a great idea. Make sure it's not a "bitch cup" session.
- Find a common goal or connection. From exercise to weight loss, sports, reading, and other ways to come together, groups can transform school culture if the key messages are upbeat and forward-thinking.

🤍 Avoid the doldrums of the same old thing! Students are coming into our classes and schools with skill sets that are constantly changing. Adjusting to those skills is part of mastering our craft, enjoying learning new things, and being willing to model for our students that we take learning seriously. Innovations may also create fantastic opportunities, even if we may not see them initially. With all the different learning curves that influence how students learn, our sanity depends on developing new teaching methods.

♡Be honest with yourself! It's impossible to enjoy your job if you hate your job. Take a second and read that again. You have a choice if you cannot recall why you entered this career or no longer enjoy being around young people. You must be honest about how you feel. I'm not talking about having a bad day, week, or even a tough year. That happens to many of us who have worked in education and probably any other profession. I've had many tough days. But, they are far outnumbered by the great moments that happen frequently. By taking an honest look at things, it's possible to change. Ed did this, and the results were noticeable.

We constantly evaluate students' improvement and knowledge. Those same principles should apply to our careers. Even when frequent observations occur from the administration, that should never take the place of our self-analysis. As educators, loving our jobs isn't just about the content delivered, the kids we teach, or the many perks education offers. It's about having a continually evolving sense of purpose. Even if we all have different motivations, let's always remember that we can create new, exciting ways to love what we do.

You can do it:

1. What is one part of your job that you enjoy? What impact does that enjoyment have on students?
2. How do you spend quality time away from your job?

Get going:

1. In discussion with a colleague(s), come up with one thing you can do to make your jobs more rewarding.
2. Implement the suggestion and analyze how well it went.

• CHAPTER 38 •

Yeah, Dad, We're Going Fishing
(With permission from Dr. Dennis Best)

Reflection is part of our practice!
It will always be a huge contributor to the success of the students we see daily.
Story Retold by Dr. Dennis Best

I want to tell everyone a brief story. While it's short on time, I hope the value means as much to you as it did to me. My young son has always wanted to go fishing with me. But my type of fishing isn't on a creek or a lake; it's out in the ocean. In the past, I've been very hesitant to bring him because of his age. The time on a deep-sea charter can be extremely long; once the boat leaves the dock, it's not turning back. I decided that the time had come to allow my son to come with me. It was going to be about four hours on the boat, and before leaving, I identified three goals that would make the trip successful.

1. He catches a fish.
2. I catch a fish.
3. He doesn't get seasick!

When our boat finally arrived at its destination, we got to catch some fish. In deep-sea fishing, you don't cast a rod but instead just drop a line and hope that those bottom-feeding fish take the bait. It can be a test of futility but also gratifying when you get a hit on the rod. I was lucky enough to start getting some nibbles as we were fishing. While none were huge, I could see that my son was frustrated by his lack of fishing prowess. After listening to him complain and watching how much trouble he was having, I offered him some much-needed help. I suggested that he fish with my rod. (**Lesson one below: what's good for you isn't necessarily good for them**). He responded, "Dad, I don't want to catch *your* fish. I want to catch *my* fish!" Ironically, I didn't follow my advice as the principal of a school and somebody who promotes a growth mindset and student choice.

I said, "Okay, let the rod sit flat. Pull the rod back fast when you see some movement." (**Lesson two: always provide specific guidance and help so they can see success**). Of course, the task was still somewhat challenging because of my son's age. And I, an incredibly supportive dad, decided to lend a hand. Again, as previously mentioned, my son wanted none of it.

To make a long story short, not only did my son not need that much help, but he also caught the biggest fish on the trip, didn't get seasick, and I also caught a few.

After reading Dennis's story, I hope a few key points resonate:

- Students need to be empowered in their learning. This is how they develop a passion that will shape their futures.
- While we want them empowered, our job is still teaching. A considerable difference exists between letting kids "just learn" and guiding them in the process.
- Finally, ensure you listen intently and reflect on the teaching and learning process. Even when we think students understand,

they often see and hear things very differently. It's our job to provide assistance and support.

———

I'd like to thank Dr. Best for sharing his poignant story. Sometimes the very best lessons and messages come from our children. Make sure you use them wisely.

As teachers, it's common practice to think we know what students want and need. In many cases, we are correct in our assessment. That's what makes us experts. On the other hand, even when our best intentions seem right, we should always be vigilant of our audience's needs and reactions to our help. If you take a few minutes to discuss learning options with your class, the lines of communication improve. It shows the class you care about their input and may even put the onus on them to do their best work.

Watching students learn on their own marked a breakthrough in my teaching. Most times, though, we still have to guide kids in the right direction. Dr. Best's illustration shows that by some trial and error, he found that fine line between giving his son too much autonomy and none at all. That same philosophy holds in our classrooms. If we don't provide helpful, meaningful feedback and instruction, most students will miss critical areas for growth.

Dr. Best had three initial goals for his fishing trip. Accomplishing those goals wasn't easy, but he reached them by reflecting and listening to his son. Communicating and paying attention to our students forms the backbone of great relationships and a culture of trust and respect. The skill or knowledge acquisition process is rarely successful on the first try. Instead, think about the entirety of the growth that occurred. Our story with students is constantly changing, but the result should be a worthwhile experience.

You can do it:

1. How do you balance between giving too much help or none at all?
2. What steps do you take when students in your class need help understanding how to achieve mastery?

Get going:

1. During a new lesson or unit, ask students what they'd like to accomplish from their learning and how you may be able to assist them.
2. Have students work together and develop parts of a lesson or unit that they feel comfortable with and those that are challenging.

• CHAPTER 39 •
R.E.A.C.H.

No matter your role in education, there will always be unique challenges that come your way. Instead of being fearful of them, think of R.E.A.C.H. as your alternative path to success.

I've mentioned throughout the book the challenges that educators and leaders face daily. Some of those challenges are small, whereas others seem impossible. For many of us, the Covid-19 virus and lockdown created large amounts of teacher anxiety and stress. Those unforeseen events influenced our day-to-day lives. The constant changing of schedules, wearing masks, and other obstacles made our jobs even more daunting than usual. It was one of the times during my career when I questioned if I could stay in the field and my impact on young people. In hindsight, from speaking with many other professionals, it's clear that we handle hurdles differently—just as our students do. Some teachers and students loved virtual learning. It's important to remember that even when situations influence our emotions, we still should have similar goals. To simplify things, I devised an acronym: R.E.A.C.H. to help us **R**emember **E**very **A**chievement **Cr**eates **H**ope.

Remember - Over the past few years, I've taken a hard look at how being flexible with student work is vital for success. I wish I could say it was solely from my self-reflection. Unfortunately, Covid-19 forced this upon me. Initially, it was upsetting how students were late with work or needed repeated directions to get them going. Luckily, my sanity was kept in check because many students did an unbelievable job.

Like many other teachers, we love when students show excellence in the work assigned. It helps us to feel validated for all the time we put into our craft. But here is the **remember** that starts off this chapter. We must **remember** that every student is unique in motivation, ability level, family dynamics, confidence level, and willingness to take risks. Even though I knew this before Covid, it reminded me that these essential concepts greatly influence learning. Remembering to create diverse ways for students to excel isn't optional. Establishing relationships in the most challenging situations isn't optional, just as we must **remember** to keep being optimistic for our students, their families, and even us.

Every - Deeply internalizing that **every** student can learn something will make the difference between kids who may feel hopeless and those that seem inspired. Throughout our careers, we will help thousands of students. When I started teaching, it was frustrating that some students seemed to get things right away, whereas others struggled. As my career kept going, those struggles came with an essential understanding. **Every** student can learn, but they also bring exceptional skills beyond our current content. Even though we may be disappointed in how a student performs, they may do other things that might be more important. Yes, we'd love to have them do everything well. But in reality, **every** one of us should have the value of making a difference in the back of our minds.

Achievement - As you've read section three, it's clear that "reflection" is a core tenet in our field. With that reflection comes the **"achievement"** students will show. Educators know that teaching is never a static principle, or at least it shouldn't be. All of us can promote even seemingly small **achievements.** Whether a simple conversation, quiz, pay it forward, or any frequent daily **achievement**, we must create an atmosphere of pride. Students, just like adults, are more willing to take chances when they've seen the fruits of their labor. Consider that usually, those simple little daily habits mean the most. **Achievement**

for all students ensures equity in the class and fosters an environment that students want to be part of.

Create - Over fifty years of being a student and a teacher have led me to believe that how we **"create"** the atmosphere of classroom instruction is paramount to students' happiness and success. It may seem extreme to many that the word "create" is what I've used to describe teaching. If we think about it, though, so much learning is about the opportunities educators create. When it comes to building connections, there are no limits to creative ways to foster relationships. The educator who **creates** a dynamic environment is one step ahead of someone who doesn't. The educator who **creates** a place where student acceptance is the rule—not the exception—will always have a welcoming classroom. Finally, an educator who **creates** an exploratory zone of risk-taking is the type of educator who will leave a lasting positive impression on their students.

Hope - **HOPE** is a guiding principle behind our teaching. No matter the student, sharing a message of **hope** raises the spirit and fosters a sense of "we can do this!" When we are trying to inspire **hope** in our students, here is something you might consider saying; "**Hope** is something that nobody can take away from you. **Hope** helps us get through the most challenging moments and pushes us to be better in those extraordinary times. **Hope** never gets old and is always a provider of the best yet to come."

You can do it:

1. How does your classroom or school use R.E.A.C.H. or a similar message to instill a culture of excellence?
2. How do you ensure that "hope" is a consistent message in your classroom?

Get going:

1. Come up with a word or acronym that connects your students to your passion for teaching
2. Ask students what words come to mind when being in your classroom.

• CHAPTER 40 •

FEARLESS

Mr. Shapiro, thank you for always making me smile, putting me in a good mood,
and believing in me. Have a great summer!
Sereniti Cronk (2022)

Before I get to how we have to embrace and help kids/staff to develop that fearless attitude, there is a brief story that I want to dedicate to Sereniti. We'd begun our virtual learning in the fall of 2020. Students and staff had the summer to prepare for the unknown of new teaching and learning. When the first class started, I vividly recall entering our first Google Meet and thinking, "Wow, that's a ton of kids with their cameras off!" Through lots of prodding and positive talk, some students found their way to put them on. I'd mention, "Listen, everyone, I know this is challenging, but just give it a try." I thought forcing kids to put on their cameras would be foolish, stressing them out even more. But talking to an icon was frustrating for those who've embraced this experience.

On one of the following days, Sereniti, whom I'd had the previous year, came to an asynchronous session that I offered. We had not developed a positive relationship in the past, even though I tried to make a difference to no avail. As we started to chat, I said, "I know it's tough to have your camera on, but I want you to be a little "fearless" and give it a shot. She put it on, and I immediately said, "Awesome, so great to see you in class!" She smiled and said, "thank you." As our conversation came to a close, I said, "What is our word from now on?" She said, "fearless!" Since that day, I've noticed a great change in how much she participates, smiles, and just gets involved.

This isn't by luck. By inspiring our students to be "fearless" in taking those risks that may be initially intimidating, we build skills that are life-long and meaningful. Even if it's time intensive and you feel frustrated, the results are truly worth it. Sereniti, thank you for being "fearless" and a great example of what's possible when you try new things.

Whether during the pandemic or in our current state of education, we all have fears of the unknown. How to use new technology? What happens when mistakes occur (like when my camera froze with 26 kids staring at me) or even something as simple as not knowing how to do a task you've never tried before? Taking on that fearless attitude isn't easy. There will always be reasons not to be fearless. Here are a few ways to make it happen for those willing to try it.

Be patient - It's easy to aim for the fences when trying to either become "fearless" or to inspire it in students. My experience tells me that getting that initial step in the right direction is critical. Sereniti started with the task of just putting her camera on. It's led to other fantastic steps that may not have happened if I'd said, "I need you to put your camera on, get more involved, ask more questions, etc." That probably would have stopped any possible progress and even led to a regression in her progress. The same things apply to us. I've learned that trying to get everything right is a recipe for complete frustration. Instead, I've focused on one thing at a time.

Know your goal - My goal was simple. Get her to feel comfortable with her camera on. It's challenging to think about what we'd like to accomplish. That's understandable, considering the many responsibilities we all face. But, again, you might get frustrated and quit without an initial goal to strive for. Picking a beginning S.M.A.R.T. goal that is attainable can be very helpful. It's no different from the many specific goals we always set for ourselves.

Look for feedback - When it comes to being "fearless," the positive affirmations we get from others are essential. Sereniti mentioned how happy she was with her camera on and the conversation we had. This is similar to other students who are grateful you've helped them on a new positive path. Likewise, colleagues appreciate having their voices heard and especially gravitate to others who share successful ideas.

Avoid the "it won't work" mantra - We've all had moments where doubt has entered our mind about trying something new. It's just human nature to have those fears. The practice it takes to overcome those fears isn't easy. The mindset we start with will make or break the "fearless" attitude. Again, this sounds like pie-in-the-sky thinking, but going into something new and believing in yourself and others works. Think about the power that motivation, teamwork, and inspiration play in many goals we set. Our classrooms, schools, and communities are no different. The internal belief systems we have directly influence whether we push forward or quit.

Accept being "fearless" - I won't lie, watching Sereniti and others embrace the simple acts of a camera made many tough days manageable. Having students take those "fearless" steps is enormous. I guarantee you'll be grinning ear-to-ear when you see the power in a "fearless" mindset for yourself and your students. Accept, and embrace it.

I can't think of many great things that happened during the Covid crisis. It was incredibly challenging to teach and work in such unique circumstances. But connecting with Sereniti, when the year before seemed hopeless, showed both of us that taking those initial risks was well worth it. I look back on a few of these "fearless" moments and cherish the power they've given students. They have also helped me to challenge my fears of failure. I'm hoping you'll take the tips above as guidelines and become fearless on your own.

You can do it:

1. What is something you've done that has made you proud of being "fearless?"
2. How have you helped your students to develop a "fearless" attitude?

Get going:

1. Try something new in your class or lessons that may be intimidating. Write down how it felt when you gave it a try.
2. Pick a goal for a student or class that will inspire them to see the power of being fearless.

Notes

◦ CHAPTER 41 ◦

We are wrapping it all up

Being a teacher is a lesson in humility. Even when we think we have it all figured out, there will always be some way to better our students' lives.

W hen I reflect on starting as a business major in college, being a personal trainer, and even managing a clothing store, it gives me pause at how writing this book came together. It started as a bunch of jumbled post-it notes and became an endeavor encapsulating my 30+ years in education. During and after writing each chapter, I'd read what the draft looked like. Frequently, my thoughts came back to how fortunate we are to have the opportunity to share so many moments in front of students. The constant reflection and writing forced me to question my practice. Even after writing the book, I'm still a work in progress with all that I've written.

You might see this as a problem, but it's more like a chance to keep improving and evaluating the work that happens each day. With that opportunity comes the understanding that this book was only possible with a passion for our field. Education, at its core, should be a profession that provides endless chances for growth.

There have been many instances, while exercising with students, joking in class, or walking through the hallways, that I can't help but smile at our generation of upcoming adults. Some people may find that idealistic, but those ideas are based on experiences.

My initial goals when writing the book were that it would be: easy to read, easy to understand, and usable right away for everyone. Most importantly, it should have provided a positive, inspirational look at education. Whatever your reaction, I hope it's met some or even all those goals. Hopefully, you already use some of what I've described. If you have, that's awesome; keep up that great work, and now pick little tidbits that might improve the meaningful ways you impact students. If you have yet to try any of these ideas, consider choosing one or two from each section and see how they work. They might provide a spark of innovation or passion in your teaching. Even if you try something and don't like it, you've still learned the importance of not standing in quicksand. Nobody can promise you that everything you try will make a difference, but it seems clear that your students will get nothing new if you try nothing new. Teaching is never meant to be static.

Writing this book has prompted me to question my practice in the most positive of ways. I use what I've written consistently. But in those instances where the little details sometimes become a struggle, having them available as a guide motivates me to keep at it. I'm hoping that message resonates with each of you.

I've listed some contact information if you'd like to reach me for questions, professional development, speaking engagements, or just to chat. *Thank you for reading Dream Big: Stories and Strategies for a Successful Classroom!* Here is one final quote, student reflection, and thank you to close it out.

> *Whatever your role in education, students need our passion, energy, and hopeful attitude. Each moment with students is another chance to make a difference in their lives. Your guidance is why they follow in our footsteps."*

— Craig Shapiro

Craig

Twitter: @Shapiro_WTHS | @Positively_Well | #teachpos

Instagram: @wtcccoach

TikTok: Chatting with Shap

Boomerizzy@gmail.com

https://cmsdreambig.com/

A Few Final Words From Laura

Craig Shapiro. Quite a name, right? One you could never forget. When his name comes up, so many great things come to mind, the most distinct being what a fantastic guy he has been throughout the five years I have known him. When I was younger, my twin brother and I decided...well... we were signed up by our mother to go to a summer cross-country camp at William Tennent High School (thanks, mom...). At only ten years old, our endurance was not very good, and neither was our mindset. We dreaded going to the camp rather than being at home, climbing trees, or messing around at the park. But, whatever mom said goes. My brother Frank and I pushed through most of it, but sometimes we lost our patience or strength to finish the practice. We wanted to give up after only a few days, despising the long distances we had to race in, no matter the weather. However, one day at camp, I was beating myself up for not beating my time, and I sat and sulked by the fences, gulping down water to help hide my true emotions. Suddenly, one of the coaches approached me and began talking with me. I told him how I felt, and he gave me a pep talk, reminding me that the times don't matter, that the only thing that matters is that I was having fun and making myself a better athlete. Who was the coach, you might ask? Why it was Mr.Shapiro himself.

Fast forward five years later, I now have Mr. Shapiro as a teacher for Health, one of my favorite periods in my roster. Arriving at Shap's class is always so great. He always has some great tunes and a positive attitude that can flip anyone's bad day around. Mr.Shapiro is the teacher who always looks out for you and cares for his students. He is not your average teacher. He wants what is best for his students: to live a happy life and not stress themselves because of "busy work." Being a sophomore has been rough, with stress and anxiety rising and falling as days go on and never going a week without crying over something school-related. However, whenever I feel down, I know 100% that Mr.Shapiro is there for me, regardless of the situation. His teaching style is like no other, engaging his students in an active-learning-based curriculum with real-life lessons every student should know and understand. Mr. Shapiro is a great man and teacher, but most importantly, a true friend who cares for his students like his own kids. Mr.Shapiro has the biggest heart in the world, never letting you down, always there to pick you up when you stumble. Don't believe me? Spend 40 minutes with this man, and I promise you, your life will be changed. Thank you, Mr.Shapiro, for being the most understanding teacher around.

Laura Orzehoski

Class of 2020

The journey of completing a book is rarely easy, especially if it's the first one. It's impossible to list all the names of adults and students who've made this book possible. Each chapter was inspired by the thousands of folks who've touched my teaching career. With that said, let's start with my children, Alana and Cole. They were often my somewhat "sarcastic, complaining teens" who helped me understand how students think. Frequently, they'd shoot me a look when I asked a specific question or responded with a "not again, dad!" However, I'm grateful for their honesty, even if I disagreed with them!

There was no way I could spend hours, days, weeks, and months on a book without the support of my spouse. While I didn't always tell her, I'm grateful that my wife, Kyle, supported this endeavor. She helped me reflect on my work without being overly critical. Also, her ability to relate as another educator helped me see a different perspective on my writing.

Another huge thank you to my incredible friend, Michael Sandler. I can't think of another person with whom I've shared more ideas than he. Michael isn't just a fantastic friend; he is an outstanding educator. Through our hundreds of conversations, he has shaped much of my teaching. His organizational skills, creative juices, and desire to make a difference for kids inspired me to follow his lead. Most important of all, as it relates to this book, is his honest opinions about many chapters.

You can make many connections with your colleagues when you teach for three-plus decades. I've been blessed more than I deserve. My elementary, middle, and high school years allowed me to be around many incredible educators. It's impossible to name all the folks who've helped me in the writing journey, even when most don't realize it. Having spent most of my career at William Tennent High School, I've been surrounded by educators who genuinely make a positive difference. They should be recognized for the tremendous impact they have on students. I'll be mentioning a few names shortly, but I wanted to thank the entire school for bringing your incredible talents each day. The students and families are lucky to have you in their lives!

As a follow-up to the above note of thanks, I'm grateful that Ms. Janna Francis has been a considerable part of this book. Not only is Janna a dear friend, but she is also a genuinely fantastic artist. When I asked her to help with the artwork, I knew her talent would bring incredible depth to book. Janna's creative imagination, positivity, and authenticity always inspire me to improve. I feel beyond blessed to have her as part of *Dream Big*. Janna, "thank you for your time, commitment, willingness to share, and our amazing friendship! You rock!"

Now for another individual who has made this happen. To Nancy King Berkovitz, my dear friend, fantastic colleague, and one of the kindest/funniest people I know. Thank you for making *Dream Big* happen. While I know you'll say otherwise (with a snarky remark), the book would not have been done without your guidance, writing skills, and constant feedback. I mean that! I appreciate your time, energy, skillful way of shortening my run-on sentences, and a hundred other details beyond this book. I admire, respect, and trust you beyond just being a colleague. You're a friend who has made a positive difference in my life!

When you write a book, a publisher has to believe in you! I want to thank Sarah Thomas, founder of Edumatch Publishing, who is funny, clever, and all things that make education awesome. When we first chatted, it was apparent that Sarah had a passion for teaching that was uniquely positive. Also, Mandy Froehlich has guided me through this process. Her time, energy, support, and patience made things seamless and never stressful. My editor Judy Arzt did a fantastic job of being patient, enthusiastic, and timely with her many corrections. She made the transition from manuscript to book seamless and positive. I'm grateful for her knowledge and wisdom.

Finally, to the thousands of students. Thank you for showing me the power of connecting with children and teens. While I can't say that every day was perfect, the vast majority have made my life fulfilling and eventful in the best sort of way. Watching students in the hallways laughing, "yelling, "SHAP," coming into my room while I'm teaching, or the countless other tidbits have made my career something I wouldn't change. Our exceptional students make the world a better place. From my heart, thank you!!

About the Author

Craig has been in the field of education for over 30 years. He has taught Health and Physical Education at all grade levels, coached many sports, participated in numerous extracurricular events, led professional training, and been active in different committees throughout his career. He teaches at William Tennent High School in Bucks County, Pennsylvania, where he is a co-coordinator of the school's Strength Club and one of the Social-Emotial Learning Liaisons. Craig has also presented at conferences about wellness, SEL, and developing culture in the classroom. He frequently shares wellness ideas and strategies on social media and hosts a Twitter chat called #teachpos on Sunday nights at 7:30 p.m. est.

Craig has a true passion for wellness, with a special love for all types of strength training. He currently has numerous state records and holds the national record for his age and weight in power-lifting.

Craig has been married to his wife, Kyle, for 26 years. They have two children, Alana and Cole, and two dogs, Bella and Zoey.

www.ingramcontent.com/pod-product-compliance
Lightning Source LLC
Chambersburg PA
CBHW051613120626
46551CB00014B/1777